I HATE THE
DALLAS
COWBOYS

And Who Elected Them
America's Team Anyway?

I HATE THE DALLAS COWBOYS

And Who Elected Them America's Team Anyway?

BERT RANDOLPH SUGAR, *Editor*

ST. MARTIN'S GRIFFIN ⚮ New York

A THOMAS DUNNE BOOK.
An imprint of St. Martin's Press.

Design by Bonni Leon-Berman

Library of Congress Cataloging-in-Publication Data

Sugar, Bert Randolph.
    I hate the Dallas Cowboys, and who elected them America's Team anyway? / Bert Sugar.
        p. cm.
    ISBN 0-312-16868-3
    1. Dallas Cowboys (Football team)—Miscellanea.   I. Title.
GV956.D3S85 1997
796.332'64'097642812—dc21   97-16595
                                                                  CIP

First St. Martin's Griffin Edition: October 1997

10   9   8   7   6   5   4   3   2   1

This volume is dedicated to everyone who has ever rooted against the Dallas Cowboys or cringed at hearing them called America's Team. It is our small contribution to the taking of America back from Dallas and returning it to all fans everywhere.

CONTENTS

FOREWORD

Enough! Enough already with that "America's Team" crap!

Every time I hear the Dallas Cowboys referred to as America's Team, I feel like tossing my cookies—preferably somewhere in the direction of Dallas.

Like Peter Finch in the movie *Network,* "I'm mad as hell and I'm not going to take it anymore!" I'm not going to take having the Cowboys constantly rammed down my throat as America's Team. I'm not going to take having the rest of the NFL relegated to second-class citizenship because some ill-mannered, beer-burping Bubbas—with typical Texas hubris—think they're better than the rest of us. And I'm not going to take having those clowns parading around with that little star on their helmets claiming to represent all of us.

After all, who in purple mountains' majesty elected them "America's Team" anyway? Did you have a vote? I know I certainly didn't. But there they are, calling themselves America's Team, just as Moammar Khadafy and Saddam Hussein elected themselves "dictators for life." That's the American way? That's—as they say down in Texas—bullspit!

After two decades of their calling themselves America's Team, you'd think they'd be embarrassed. Especially in light of their recent acts of insufferable vulgarity and other acts against the senses too numerous to mention. But no, those arrogant blowhards, masters of the overkill, have now begun to believe their own press notices. And there they go again, calling their 1997 highlight film—can you believe this?—*America's Team Forever.*

That did it! I can't take this nonsense any longer. Something must be done to counteract this "America's Team" myth that has crept into our cultural consciousness. It's time to do something to give the vast majority of fans who do not root for the Cowboys a chance to stand up and be counted.

And so it was that I decided the time was ripe for a book called *I Hate the Dallas Cowboys, and Who Elected Them America's Team Anyway?* But rather than giving you just one man's take, I have found twenty like-minded former players and current writers to share my podium and vent their feelings about the team that dares to call itself America's Team.

The combined efforts of what may, in years to come, be known as the Anti-Cowboy Twenty will hopefully serve not only as a rallying cry but as a digestive curative for the rest of us who have been served a steady diet of this "America's Team" garbage. For most of us, to know them is to loathe them, their continued success on the sports pages and their frequent appearances on the police blotter making them The Team You Love to Hate.

The Cowboys have become latter-day successors to the New York Yankees atop the fans' "hate meter." But the Yankees weren't really hated; their success was. After all, how could you hate some of the most lovable characters this side of the Seven Dwarfs: Casey Stengel, Yogi Berra, Mickey Mantle, Whitey Ford, et al.? Or earlier, Joe DiMaggio, Babe Ruth, Lou Gehrig, etc.? All the Yankees begat for their continued successes were a few catcalls of "Break Up the Yankees" and one book, Douglass Wallop's *The Year the Yankees Lost the Pennant,* the basis for the play and movie *Damn Yankees.* The Cowboys, however, have never had lovable characters. In fact, if anything, they make you wonder how they can get eleven men out on a work-release program every weekend.

You would think this would be an embarrassment to all. All, that is, except their followers, who suffer no such embarrassment. But then, how are you going to embarrass someone from Texas?

Texans—and, by extension, Dallas Cowboy fans—are used to being the butt of jokes, some going all the way back almost to the time Father Adam first heard the rush of the apple salesmen. One of the first came when General Phil Sheridan was asked what he thought of Texas. He replied, "If I owned two plantations and one was located in Texas and the other in Hell, I'd rent out the one in Texas and live in the other one." Throughout the next century, others checked in with equally biting remarks. One visiting senator described the area as "a place with more cows and less milk, more rivers and less water, and you can look farther and see less than anywhere else on earth." And one comedian said, "It's interesting to see what they call rivers in Texas. Up in Oregon, they've got basements with more water."

And here's one that's been circulating recently:

> Saint Peter was sitting in front of the Pearly Gates, clipboard in hand, awaiting the arrival of new applicants for admission to Heaven. The first applicant showed up, and after going through all the

entrance requirements and finding that the applicant had passed them, Saint Peter proudly an-
nounced, "Welcome to Heaven." And then, before
stepping aside to allow entry, he said, "But before
you go, I must ask you one more question: What's
your IQ?" The new entrant answered, "One eighty,"
and Saint Peter said, "Before you enter, please sit
down a second and let's discuss Einstein's Theory
of Relativity." In a little while another applicant
showed up, and Saint Peter repeated the process,
again announcing that the applicant had passed all
the requirements. And again he asked the new entrant, "What's your IQ?" "One twenty" was the reply. "Good," said Saint Peter. "Let's sit down and
discuss the laws of supply and demand." Soon
there was another knock on the Pearly Gates, and
Saint Peter again went through the same proce-
dure. After checking the third applicant through,
Saint Peter asked, "What is your IQ?" The third answered, "Sixty." After a moment's hesitation, Saint
Peter finally said, "How 'bout them Cowboys?"

There are thousands more, and although Texans have
come to view it as their inalienable right to be picked
on, they are overly sensitive about the slings and arrows
hurled in their direction. Rather than pay them "no
never mind," they hide their hurt behind an us-versus-
them defensive mentality, almost as if their manhood
were at stake. The result has been a posture of self-
importance, one that has manifested itself in an over-
blown sense of superiority, turning all Texans into
blowhards and braggarts. After all, preening like pouter
pigeons, they will tell you 136 valiant men held off an
army of 15,000 for four days at the Alamo, but that that
"candy-ass" Paul Revere had to run for help.

Besides their blowhardiness is the fact that Texans, in the words of Molly Ivins, are "more than passin' strange." After all, she notes, it's a place where you can get a five-year sentence for murdering someone, and a ninety-nine-year one for smoking pot. Where it's "all rat" (as in *right*) to drink and drive. And where there's nothing more obscene than "gummint" gun control.

Put them all together and, to the average "rat-thinkin'" Texan, the degenerate goings-on and the running undertide of scandal that engulfs the current edition of the Cowboys are just part of the local landscape, harmless little perversions. And the stuff of which a real "America's Team" is made. After all, "Cowboys will be 'Boys."

To hear them tell it—and to hear them, you've got to listen closely, their words arranging themselves into some small stagger at a passable version of the mother tongue, turning the word *boys* into *bhoys*—their "Cowbhoys" are America's Team 'cause they represent America.

"Sumbitch," as they say down "thar," that makes a strange sort of sense. But many things make strange sense down thar, especially when they come out of the mouths of Bubbas who believe that "Chanukah" is some sort of duck call.

In Dallas, a town where there are over two dozen different churches, there is only one true religion: the Dallas Cowboys. And every Sunday during the season they worship at the altar of "Our Lady of the Latter Day Victory." Which is not so far-fetched when you consider that Texans once embraced "Drop-Kick Me, Jesus, Through the Goalposts of Life" as their anthem.

Like Saint Paul condescending to humor the superstitious Corinthians, the Dallas Cowboys have taken it upon themselves to humor these poor lost souls, still sensitive over being labeled the City of Hate after the JFK assassination. And the Cowboy parishioners have responded in kind, "Amen-ing" in response to every passing—and running—triumph over what they perceive as the forces of evil. To them, their 'Bhoys can do no wrong. And any sorry sumbitch who thinks different is un-American to think anything but good thoughts about "America's Team."

And how are you going to argue with that kind of reasoning, coming as it does from those a little light in their gray matter?

Molly Ivins once wrote: "To define Dallas is to add a whole new humongous dimension to bad." The twenty players and writers in this book think that extends to the Dallas Cowboys as well and have defined the Cowboys in as many different ways as possible. All bad. And while *I Hate the Dallas Cowboys and Who Elected Them America's Team Anyway?* is not necessarily a Dallas-bashing party, it will serve as one for all who wish to join.

America's Team? Bullspit!

Bert Randolph Sugar
June 7, 1997

I HATE THE
DALLAS
COWBOYS

And Who Elected Them America's Team Anyway?

INTRODUCTION

A History of the Dallas Cowboys

If the Cowboys Aren't America's Team, Whose Team Are They Anyway?

TO UNDERSTAND WHAT MAKES a Cowboy fan, you've got to understand Dallas first and then the Cowboys. And to do so, you've got to start at the beginning, all the way back to the 1840s, when a settler named John Neely Bryan staked his claim in the middle of nowhere. For miles around he could see nothing and nobody. And so he promptly named his newfound home after a nobody, one of the most undistinguished Vice Presidents of all time, one George Mifflin Dallas. Dallas had been in office when Congress admitted Texas to the union in 1845. Had but three percent of the populace in the 1844 election cast their votes for Henry Clay instead of Dallas's running mate, James K. Polk, then the Vice President at the time of Texas's admission to the union would not have been Dallas but Clay's Vice Presidential running mate, Theodore Frelinghuysen. And Dallas would have been "Frelinghuysen," the "Big F" instead of the "Big D." Which would have been perfect.

Anyway, Dallas, not Frelinghuysen, it was. And for the next century or so it went on its merry who-gives-a-damn-let's-pop-open-a-beer way. In 1937 the Chamber of Commerce proudly published a pamphlet extolling the city as one of "300,000 citizens, 60 miles of paved roads and acres of large shade trees." It was also a "City of Churches" and a college-football town on Saturday afternoons and a high-school football town on Friday nights.

In 1952 the NFL voyaged, Columbus-like, into this virgin pro territory, transferring the moribund New York Yankees franchise to Dallas and renaming them the Dallas Texans. But although the team was stocked with name—and soon-to-be-name—players like Buddy Young, Frank Tripucka, Hank Lauricella, George Taliaferro and two future Hall of Famers, Gino Marchetti and Art Donovan, the fans in Dallas showed about as much interest in the Texans as they did in the municipal bond interest rate. After just four games—including three in the cavernous Cotton Bowl—the owners threw in the towel and returned control of the franchise to the league. For the rest of the season, the Texans were gypsies roaming the land. By the next season the franchise had moved to Baltimore, and pro football in Dallas became a faint memory.

Eight years later, Fate gave birth again when the NFL placed a new franchise in Dallas. Actually, it was less a natural birth than artificial insemination, this offspring of pro football fathered by the millionaire son of a Dallas billionaire, Lamar Hunt.

A local dreammaker, Hunt had long envisioned a professional team in Dallas. Early in 1959 he had petitioned the NFL to buy the Chicago Cardinals franchise and move it to Dallas. Rebuffed, he next petitioned for a new franchise in Dallas, with the same result. Denied admission to the closed fraternity of the NFL, Hunt did what any self-respecting millionaire would do: He went out and bought himself a league of his own, the American Football League, with a franchise in Dallas called the Texans.

With the advent of the new league, the NFL, which had not been open to the idea of expansion before, hurriedly voted to head off Hunt's colonization of Dallas by awarding an expansion franchise to another Texas millionaire, Clint Murchison. Suddenly, a town that had previously demonstrated an inability to support a single pro football team was now crowded to overflowing with two.

Although the franchise wouldn't be officially awarded to Murchison until late January of 1960, with a poker player's daring, he set up a shadow operation in the law offices of co-owner Bedford Wynne months before. There a skeletal crew—consisting of general manager Tex Schramm, player personnel chief Gil Brandt, and secretary Ilene Gish—performed the unenviable task of establishing an NFL beachhead in Dallas while holding off the AFL's all-out assault.

The American Football League fired the first shot of the war on November 22, 1959, when it held its first draft. The Dallas franchise had the first pick and selected local hero Don Meredith of Southern Methodist. Fearing Meredith would be lost, "Papa Bear" George Halas, one of the founding fathers of the NFL, traded the Bears' rights to Meredith to Dallas for a later draft choice. And although the NFL had not yet officially recognized the Murchison entry, that very same week Dallas signed Meredith to a personal services contract immediately after SMU's final 1959 regular-season game.

Dallas would acquire one other player by the same route—Don Perkins of the University of New Mexico, who was signed as a favor to Senator Clinton Anderson of New Mexico, who sat on the newly formed expansion team's board of directors.

They were to be the only two, however, as very soon Murchison and Company found that such gifts of charity as being granted a new franchise came encumbered with strings to tie, bills to pay, and mortgages to assume. After the signing of Meredith and Perkins, they now had to depend upon the beneficence of the league to stock the rest of their roster. And of beneficence there was none, the NFL even excluding Dallas from its 1960 collegiate draft. Instead, for the $600,000 in hard Eisenhower bucks Murchison & Co. had ponied up, all they were entitled to participate in was something called an "Equalization Draft." This was, in actuality, a misnomer since those there for the surplus taking consisted of only three players per club available after each of the twelve existing teams had frozen twenty-five men on their rosters. And most of those available were the stuff of which unsungs are made.

With such slim pickings, Schramm and Brandt came to the realization that franchise-building did not lie in this direction; it was like trying to make bricks without straw. So they turned instead to the free-agent market. Xeroxing every NFL contract he could get his hands on, Schramm handed them over to Brandt, along with a mandate to scour the countryside with a missionary zeal in his search for free agents.

Brandt's progress, slow at first, finally began to bear fruit. The first olive out of the proverbial jar was halfback Jake Crouthamel of Dartmouth. After a bidding war with the AFL, represented by Frank Leahy, Brandt signed Crouthamel to a contract for $8,500. Brandt immediately called Schramm to tell him of his good fortune. All Schramm asked was "How much?" not "Who?"

There would be other free-agent signings. But still, when the team gathered for the first time at its training facility at Pacific University in Forest Grove, Oregon, it was, at best, a threadbare group. The talent was inexpressibly dreary. Only four had any name recognition: two who had been persuaded to postpone retirement, quarterback Eddie LeBaron and linebacker Jerry Tubbs; one who had been obtained in the Equalization Draft, end Frank Clarke; and Meredith. The rest of the roster could be taken to the Missing Persons Bureau for identification.

But two names would become as familiar over the coming years as the very name *Dallas* itself: the head coach, Tom Landry, and the team name, the Cowboys.

Landry was a local Dallas favorite, having played at the University of Texas. For the previous four seasons he had been the defensive coordinator for the Eastern Conference champion New York Giants. Now, just as Vince Lombardi, the Giants' offensive coordinator, had the season before, Landry left the Giants to take over as a head coach, signing with the Cowboys immediately after the 1959 championship game.

The name would come later, just in time for the league to print it in its preseason literature. Originally the franchise had been called the Dallas Steers, the idea of part-owner Bedford Wynne, who was a graduate of the University of Texas and was playing off the school's nickname, the Longhorns. When Schramm returned from the 1960 Rome Olympics, however, he turned up his nose at the name and changed it to the Cowboys. And, like all of Schramm's ideas, it was written in stone. Cowboys it was and Cowboys it would be.

That first year served as a just-getting-acquainted year—as in getting acquainted with new teammates and with Tom Landry's playbook, a tome thick enough to stock a sectional bookshelf. Its curriculum was a wide one, but one partial to a single-minded orthodoxy: Have the offense take advantage of the other team's defense, find its weaknesses, and exploit them, thus making great demands on the opponent.

Landry demanded that his players excel in the mechanical perfection of their game. And in the mechanical execution of his game plan. And so it was that every day before practice, to make sure they were on the same page, he would conduct a chalk talk in the manner of someone constantly touching fresh paint to see if it is dry—his way of ensuring his system was being absorbed by his charges.

In the very first such team meeting, Landry stood at the blackboard snapping off his formations like a light switch. As quickly as his right hand drew Xs and Os, his left would just as feverishly erase them. He called on Meredith to come to the board and draw the same strongside-right formation against a 4–3 defense he had just diagrammed. Twitching all over, Meredith approached the blackboard, his eyes looking like they had just come out of their sockets. He had not the foggiest what Landry had just diagrammed.

At SMU, Meredith had played in a freelance offense, one that had required nothing more of him than lining up in a spread and then either running or passing. That was it. Now, alternating with Eddie LeBaron at quarterback, he was required to learn a completely new system, a complicated one employing numbers and colors for hundreds of formations. It would take time.

Before a preseason game against the Giants in Louisville, Landry went through his normal Xs and Os chalk talk, accompanying his hieroglyphics with sound bites:

"When Huff edges up to fill the gap this way . . . you go like this . . ." The coach would add emphasis to his words by slashing his chalk on the blackboard. "When he goes like that . . ." Another swoosh of chalk. "And when Sam goes this way . . ." The chalk zigged! "You go that way . . ." The chalk zagged! The coach was anticipating moves that Giant linebacker Sam Huff would make in a particular situation in a defense of Landry's own design. And all the while Meredith sat there nodding his head, not sure whether to laugh or cry.

Come the game and Meredith called a fullback wedge, a play designed to work between the tackles. Barking out signals, he noticed Huff edging up to the line. When Meredith called, "Ah . . . 31 . . . ," Huff answered with a step to his right while Giant tackle Rosey Grier adjusted his stance. "Ah . . . 31 . . . brown right, 34 slant . . ." Meredith fumphered. Huff moved again while Andy Robustelli and Dick Modzelewski also altered their positions. "Ah . . . 34 . . . red light . . ." Meredith now hemmed and hawed, and Huff once again shifted. "Ah . . . 34 . . . 22 . . . EGO . . . pop . . . ah . . . ah . . . shoot! TIME OUT!!" Meredith finally shouted and trotted over to the sidelines, having plumb forgotten what he was supposed to do, while his teammates grabbed their sides to keep from falling over in laughter.

After a hasty consultation with Landry—less a discussion than a dressing-down—Meredith took his position over center again. But Meredith's signal calling was no better the second go-round, except this time, during the "mux-ip," a frustrated Huff jumped offsides, giving Dallas a first down. And in so doing, he kept the Dallas drive, such as it was, alive. The result was a Dallas score and their first win. Ever.

That would prove to be not only the highlight of the

Cowboys' preseason, but of their entire maiden season. It was a season so dismal that had they been dominoes, they would have come up double zero. In fact, they almost did, underwhelming all but one of the twelve teams they played. The only non-loss on their record came in a next-to-last-game tie against the Giants. They were so bad, someone even suggested that if the quarterback had been sitting on his helmet, the other team would have intercepted it.

The Cowboys weren't faring much better at the gate, either. Forced to share the town's allegiance with the Texans—who, at least by AFL standards, had fielded a creditable team—the Cowboys were forced to share that temple of Southwest Conference football, the Cotton Bowl, with their crosstown rivals as well. Here again they lost. Like gunfighters maneuvering for position at the OK Corral, the two teams drew coat-hanger tags for open dates at the Cotton Bowl. The Texans won the preferred Sunday playing dates, including the biggest football date of the year: the carnival weekend of the annual Texas-Oklahoma game.

Helped in no small measure by "papering" the house with giveaways, the Texans managed to outdraw the Cowboys in a head-to-head count, but both teams played in relative obscurity. It was becoming increasingly obvious that Dallasites, brought up on Saturday football games and Sunday church services, thought it sacrilegious to consider the alternatives. And so the alternatives lost heavily.

For the next couple of seasons the Cowboys continued to struggle, their wins few and far between. Off-the-field circumstances, however, would prove to be more important to the Cowboys' fortunes than their won-lost record.

The first occurred because Schramm and Brandt refused to accept the situation as unalterable. Believing that the door to opportunity rarely needs a picked lock, merely the right combination to open it, they found that right combination in the form of the collegiate draft. Looking for players who exuded the essential qualities they were looking for, they cut them out of the herd. It was a formula that led them to their first-ever draft choice, a quick, strong defensive end out of TCU, Bob Lilly. It worked again in 1962 when they grafted on the talents of two more newcomers, defensive end George Andrie and end Pettis Norman. Despite their mediocre efforts on the field, the Cowboys were stockpiling talent for the future. Talent that would pay off, handsomely.

The other event was even more essential to the ultimate success of the Cowboys as a franchise. After a three-year fight for fan acceptance, and despite having won the 1962 AFL championship, Lamar Hunt tired of playing second fiddle to the Cowboys. Believing that "two teams cannot succeed in Dallas," he took his team—lock, stock, and championship trophy—to Kansas City.

One story making the rounds at the time—later given credence by Gil Brandt—had it that in a true Western "this-town-ain't-big-enough-for-the-two-of-us" scenario, Hunt and Murchison tossed a coin, with the loser to leave. Whatever, the result was the same: The Cowboys were now the only game in town.

The fans now began returning, like pigeons over a stormy sea, to watch the Cowboys. But soon their enchantment with the team turned into disillusionment with the offense, which was playing like some of life's losing stuntmen. As the dues-paying fans' displeasure swelled along with the decibel level of their booing, Landry gave orders for only the defensive unit to be introduced in pregame ceremonies.

But even as the Cowboys, considered by many to be an outside contender for the Eastern Conference championship, continued to disappoint, Schramm and Brandt were still working their rabbit's foot successfully, building the foundation of strong Dallas teams to come through that Ellis Island of pro football, the college draft. In 1963, the Cowboys added tackle Tony Liscio and linebacker Lee Roy Jordan; in 1964, defensive back Mel Renfro and futures Roger Staubach and Bob Hayes; and in 1965, tackle Ralph Neely, defensive end Jethro Pugh, and quarterback Craig Morton. The Cowboys now had so much young talent it was available at a discount.

By 1965 observers could see the Cowboys' star rising. Destined, like water, to find their own level, the Cowboys leveled their won-lost record at 7–7, finishing second in the Eastern Conference and winning the right to play the Baltimore Colts in the Playoff Bowl, a meaningless postseason game between runners-up played for the benefit of television. The highlight, as far as Dallas was concerned, came before the game when one of the Cowboys jumped up on the taping table to plead for his teammates to win the game, lamenting that the loser's share "wouldn't pay for my hotel bill." Unfortunately, his pleas went unheeded as the Colts beat the Cowboys in a blowout.

Despite the humiliating loss, the team that had started from scratch had left a calling card, one announcing they had finally "arrived." And this first appearance in a postseason game was a mere hors d'oeuvre of what was to become a steady diet of playoff appearances for the Cowboys.

Another who had arrived, finally, was Don Meredith. Coming out of the starting gate, Landry had a five-year plan for building a winner, one that called for using Eddie LeBaron at quarterback for two to three years, with Meredith then moving in. Meredith, however, had been slow to absorb Landry's complicated, regimented system, at times even rebelling against it. He complained, "The hardest thing to do with Tom's system is to believe in it." But with Landry standing firm in the ramrod conviction that comes with knowing you're always right, Meredith finally came to the realization that his coach's genius was to be served, not argued with. "You get tired of a guy being right so often . . . but Tom is right." And by becoming a believer, Meredith also became, in the process, one of the best quarterbacks in the game.

Still, with the nonchalance of a hog-caller, Meredith would often playfully put his finger in the pot and stir. One teammate remembers him bending over in the huddle on more than one occasion, singing "God Didn't Make Honky-Tonk Angels," while the rest of the team was forced to wait for ten or fifteen of the allotted thirty seconds before he would call the play. Then he would approach the line of scrimmage with a let's-go-fishing attitude, snapping his fingers and continuing to sing.

The making of a great martini is the correct mating of gin and vermouth at precisely the right moment. Like that great martini, all the elements of a great football team came together for the Cowboys in 1966. With Meredith leading the offense, helped in no small part by receiver Bob Hayes and runners Dan Reeves and Don Perkins, and with the defense leading the league in fewest yards allowed rushing and in sacks, Dallas began making up for arrearages, going over the .500 mark for the first time with a 10–3–1 record to win the Eastern Conference title.

However, 1966 would fall one yard short of being a

great year—that one yard being the one the Cowboys couldn't negotiate in the closing seconds of the NFL championship game against the Green Bay Packers. They lost 34–27, and with it a chance to go to the first Super Bowl.

The next year Dame Fortune once again allowed the Cowboys to get close enough to touch the hem of her skirt, but no farther. They repeated as Eastern Conference champions but lost again to the Packers, 21–17. The outcome was again decided in the final seconds as Green Bay's Bart Starr executed a quarterback sneak over Jerry Kramer's block in the famous "Ice Bowl."

The Cowboys continued to win black belts in disappointment the next three seasons, each ending with a loss. They seemed destined to be perennial bridesmaids, their noses pressed forever against the glass looking in. So profound was their frustration at being unable to win "The Big One" that—in a scene of anguish straight out of the Book of Job—when Baltimore's Jim O'Brien kicked a field goal to beat them in the final-final seconds of Super Bowl V, Bob Lilly yanked off his helmet and threw it farther than O'Brien's kick.

Not content to sit around and lick their wounds, the Cowboys continued to build their talent pool. As with any well-built modern machine, the Cowboys were capable of replacing each and every one of its parts and still remain the same winning machine. For every Don Meredith, who retired after the '68 season, there was a Roger Staubach or a Craig Morton. For every Don Perkins, who also left after '68, there was a Calvin Hill or a Duane Thomas. And so on and so on. If the Cowboys suffered from anything, it was an embarrassment of riches.

The Big Payoff came in 1971. After winning just four of

their first seven games, the 'Boys put together a late-season drive, leveling every opponent they faced. The scrambling Roger Staubach performed magic with passes so accurate that teammate Mel Renfro was prompted to say, "Staubach can throw a ball through a car wash and it would come out dry"; that curious piece of goods, Duane Thomas, when not contemplating his navel, Hamlet-fashion, ran the ball with devastating effect; and with the "Doomsday Defense" dominating their opponents, the Cowboys won their last ten games, including Super Bowl VI. They had finally lassoed The Big One. And forever shed their loser's image.

The Super Bowl trophy would find a home in the Cowboys' new home, Texas Stadium, in nearby Irving, which had opened earlier that same season. The 61,000-seat stadium featured a yawning hole in its roof that, one writer suggested, "would give God a chance to look down on his chosen people, the Dallas Cowboys and their fans."

God and Cowboy fans could also look down on something else the next season: the Dallas Cowboy Cheerleaders. In a state where football "in the rah"—as evidenced by the Kilgore Rangerettes and the Apache Belles—has always been part and parcel of the landscape, the Dallas Cowboy Cheerleaders outstripped anything seen before, bringing a healthy helping of "T&A" to the traditional Xs and Os. Marketed as being 56/100ths percent purer than Ivory soap, the Cheerleaders were, in the words of one reporter, "a presentation locked inside a bulletproof sugar-coating of overdone, over-made-up, over hair-sprayed, ultra-exaggerated nicey-nicey wholesomeness." To the rest of the country, watching this healthy helping of football-a-go-go jiggle and wiggle on national TV, it seemed that with their

Texas-sized measurements, the cheerleaders were no more outlandish or overdone than anything else in Dallas.

If God wasn't in his heaven and all right with the world, conditions as near to that as possible prevailed for Cowboy fans. Assured of their place in the sun, courtesy of Texas Stadium's open roof, with the Super Bowl trophy in hand and cheerleaders on the hoof, they sat back and awaited what they knew in their heart of hearts to be their inalienable right: more Super Bowl triumphs.

It was not to be. Not immediately, at any rate. In 1972 and 1973, the Cowboys reverted to form, winning eleven games each season, but not the last one. And in 1974 they failed to make the playoffs for the first time in ten years. To their fans, it was unbelievable. It was as if Santa Claus had fallen through the hole in their roof.

With the departure of such stalwarts as Bob Lilly, Walt Garrison, Calvin Hill, and Cornell Green after the 1974 season and the inevitable graying of the rest of the regulars, Cowboy parishioners believed the chances of reaching the playoffs were dead. If anything, however, the Cowboys were more alive than ever. An infusion of new blood over the previous four years had included Robert Newhouse, Billy Joe DuPree, Golden Richards, Harvey Martin, Drew Pearson, Too Tall Jones, and the Whites, Danny and Randy. With new talent and a new formation, "the Shotgun," Staubach & Co. made the soufflé rise again. They galloped through the 1975 playoffs and into the Super Bowl, only to lose to Pittsburgh.

The Cowboys were on a roll. Winning with a dismal monotony and a startling variety, the 'Boys established homesteading rights to the top of the Eastern Division and appeared in two more Super Bowls, XII and XIII.

To their fans, however, none of these accomplishments were the most important to accrue to the 'Boys during this period of prosperity. Instead, it was a title that was bestowed upon them and that their worshippers wildly embraced as their sacred due: that of being labeled America's Team.

And, despite everyone's thinking the Cowboys had dubbed themselves America's Team, the title came in one of those little serendipitous over-the-transom occurrences that always seem to happen to those who have already stepped in fresh horsepucky.

The story, dear readers, goes like this: Every year NFL Films puts together a "highlight" film for each team. A montage of the very best plays of the previous season, it is an attempt to show each team with its best cleat forward. Producer Bob Ryan, trying mightily to put the Cowboys' 1978 season in the best light, especially after their disappointing loss to Pittsburgh in Super Bowl XIII, was looking for something to ease their pain. Viewing all the footage at his disposal, Ryan noticed that there always seemed to be almost as many Cowboy jerseys in the stands at their away games as there were of the home team. It also occurred to him that the Cowboys were featured on national TV more than any other NFL team—usually as the second game of the CBS doubleheader or as the scheduled *Monday Night Football* game. To Ryan, the Cowboys were as much America's national pro football team as the Fighting Irish of Notre Dame were its national collegiate football team, the Yankees were its national baseball team, and the Celtics its national basketball team. And so it was that the 1978 Cowboys' highlight film featured announcer John Facenda, in a voice two decibels below sea level, intoning "Dallas . . . they are America's Team."

When NFL Films showed the highlight film to the Cowboy front office, Tex Schramm, who blue-penciled every-thing, not only approved the title but co-opted it. According to Ryan, Schramm believed that it was "some-thing the Cowboys could tie in to." Others, including Landry and some of players, didn't particularly care for it, believing it "made them more of a target." But Schramm paid them "no never mind," deciding it re-flected sunshine and clear weather. He put the weight of the Cowboys' marketing and publicity efforts behind it, and the title took.

And so the Cowboys became "America's Team" in much the same way that Wheaties became the Breakfast of Champions: They bought it. They bought it because it had a nice ring to it, and that was worth a considerable investment of time, effort, and cash. And the investment paid off. Soon the team the Lone Star State had taken to its bosom now extended its realm from sea to shining sea as thousands upon thousands of football fans bought the Cowboys' myth. And their NFL-licensed mer-chandise as well.

Again in 1979, the Cowboys repeated as Eastern Divi-sion champions. It had by now become one of the most utterly dependable stories in all of sports, a feat news-papers yawned at. What they didn't yawn at was the news that after the twelfth game of the season, line-backer "Hollywood" Henderson had been asked to hand in his helmet for what was called a "lackadaisical atti-tude." Pruned of its fig leaf, the truth was that Hender-son was freely using cocaine, even having sniffed some during the Super Bowl game the previous January. This precipitated a media storm. How could a team that ad-vertised itself as America's Team have a cocaine addict on its roster? The American public had a right to know.

Instead, the press should have been asking themselves why they had overlooked the many problems the Cowboys had had for years. Maybe, just maybe, it was because the Cowboys' public relations office had had a closer relationship with the local press than any other team. For years, the Cowboys had been wining and dining these guardians of truth in sport, who, in gratitude, had bought all the pious press releases handed them with all the solemnity of a Moses receiving the tablets of the law.

But even though the Cowboy front office tried to protect the private lives of their players like family jewels and project a squeaky-clean team image, occasionally some player's actions would bubble to the surface—as they had when Lance Rentzel was caught exposing himself to an underage girl. Even then the affair was airbrushed over as a "personal problem." But usually the press maintained a polite fiction of their nonexistence.

But, in that where-there's-a-will-there's-a-pill era, the Cowboys had had more than their share of walking pharmaceutical cabinets, as wonderfully depicted in former Cowboy Pete Gent's how-to guide, *North Dallas Forty*.

Gent tells one story of the "Party Hearty" Cowboys that didn't make it between the covers of his book. A Dallas offensive lineman, who shall remain nameless, while recovering from a bad LSD trip found himself up a tree, devoid of clothing. While the fire engines hurried to his fashionable Dallas home to fetch him down, the Cowboy had a momentary flash of reason. Afraid that Tom Landry, a member of the Fellowship of Christian Athletes, would cut him from the squad if he found out about this escapade, the lineman came up with an idea. He would tell the coach that he had climbed the tree "to get closer to God." Moreover, God had talked to him and told him that he would soon be named an assistant coach. When he was finally brought down, he went to face Landry, who, incredibly, bought his story. Or part of it anyway, according to Gent, who added that he never did become an assistant coach.

Somehow that little episode, like most, never made it into print. Most newspapermen, it seems, preferred to pluck out an offending eye than offend Tex Schramm and his PR flacks.

Schramm's control of everything was so complete that nothing, but nothing, went out of the Cowboy offices without his official okay. But sometimes even total control wasn't enough. Years later author Dick Whittingham wrote a book about the Cowboys and approached Schramm seeking to have a Cowboy write the foreword. Schramm, the Abominable No-man, turned down Whittingham's request, telling him, "No Cowboy would." Undaunted, Whittingham approached Roger Staubach. Courteously, Staubach heard him out and then asked, "Did Tex say we shouldn't do this?" When Whittingham answered in the affirmative, the two horizontal slits Staubach used for eyes closed in laughter and he said, "Then I'll do it."

Being a winner in sports is a transitional act; success is subject to discontinuation without further notice. And so it was with the Cowboys. After a string of nine straight playoff appearances—nineteen in twenty-one years— the fortunes of "America's Team" began to recede in the late 1980s.

Maybe it was only fitting. For despite their high-falutin' title, the Cowboys were, bottom line, merely a geographic team with fancy national pretenses. And the bottom line for the geographic area they represented was also receding. S&Ls were going belly-up, oil was on the skids, and everything else was going south. In a state where most sentiments are displayed on the bumper-sticker of the car in front of you, one that best captured the temper of the times read, PLEASE DON'T TELL MY MOTHER I'M AN OIL FIELD WORKER. SHE THINKS I'M A PIANO PLAYER IN A WHOREHOUSE. Another read, O LORD, LET ME HAVE JUST ONE MORE OIL BOOM. THIS TIME I PROMISE NOT TO PISS IT AWAY. Clint Murchison was one of those who got caught up in the Texas recession and had to sell his team. Like every other well-tooled machine in "Big D," his team was riding on its rims.

Most of the faithful viewed losing as intolerable as belching in church. So when the 1986 Cowboys endured their first losing season in twenty-two years, the faithful began to wonder if their faith had been misplaced. An undercurrent of feeling began to run among their number. And when their beloved 'Pokes went 7–8 in 1987, they began to stir a little impatiently, more sullen than mutinous. But when the team fell to 3–13 in 1988, there was a large amount of weeping and gnashing of teeth. A chorus of prayers went up: Deliver us from this famine.

Just when it seemed that the only thing that could improve the Cowboys was embalming fluid, another liquid was infused to answer the faithful's prayers: oil money, $150 million worth of it. The source of the money was Jerry Jones, an Arkansas "bidnessman" who had made his fortune in oil and gas exploration. He now had come forward to pick up the Cowboys' sputtering torch. He purchased the rights to the franchise and the stadium leases from the man who had bought them from the Murchison family, one who boasted the kind of nickname one finds only in Texas: "Bum" Bright.

Although an "Arkie," Jones immediately set about etching his name on the facade of Texas Stadium, promising in his first press conference, "I will sell my house in Little Rock and move to Dallas. My entire office and my entire business will be at the Cowboys' complex. . . . The Cowboys will be my life." After this attempt at ingratiating himself with the citizenry of Dallas, Jones went on to issue the following it's-good-to-be-king ukase: "I want to know everything there is to know, from player contracts to socks and jocks and television contracts. This is my company and I will be making all the decisions."

With his next act he really set the tone for the Jones Era: He fired Tom Landry. Dallasites were shocked. Landry was the only coach the Cowboys had ever had! In the words of Dallas sportswriter Skip Bayless, he was "held up to heavenly standards." The man who was thought to be part and parcel of the Texas landscape forever was gone with one sweep of Jerry Jones's broom, and along with him PR director Doug Todd, director of player personnel Gil Brandt, and even club president Tex Schramm, the godfather of "America's Team." The Cowboys were Jerry Jones's $150 million toy, and he was going to play with it his way, not others.'

Jones's first hire was his old University of Arkansas roommate, Jimmy Johnson, who, from 1984 through 1988, had coached the University of Miami to a 52–9 record and a national championship. Together, the two embarked on a youth movement, trading super running back Herschel Walker to the Minnesota Vikings for a moving van full of draft choices and then drafting the likes of Troy Aikman and Michael Irvin. The Cowboys were, if possible, worse than they had been the previous year, finishing the 1989 season with a 1–15 record. But they were Jerry Jones's team now, one he was creating in his own image.

Within three years, the tandem of Jones and Johnson—

with more than a little help from new players like Emmitt Smith, Alvin Harper, Russell Maryland, Jay Novacek, Leon Lett, and Charles Haley—brought the 'Boys all the way back to the top of the NFL mountain with a win over Buffalo in Super Bowl XXVII. Once again they looked down on the rest of the league. And Jerry Jones, enjoying every second as the owner of the finest team in the land—one of his own making and in his own image—could look down on his critics as well.

But all was not well in the Jones version of paradise. After leading the Cowboys to a second straight Super Bowl victory after the 1993 season, Jimmy Johnson decided one Freud egg in the front office was enough and abruptly left. Jones replaced him with Barry Switzer, whose credentials at the University of Oklahoma saw Johnson's at Miami and raised him one, at least in national championships. However, Switzer arrived with the onus of scandal from his days at OU, where he had coached a number of players whose off-field behavior was less than exemplary. Now he became coach of Jones's team, which was increasingly in need of a keeper.

The players, those self-absorbed, greed-driven, depraved godzillionaires who were constantly in search of wildlife of the two-legged variety and other expensive pursuits, were constantly in trouble, their exploits featured as often on the front page as on the sports page. Without Tex Schramm to help them hide their Hyde side, they became poster boys for the post office, not NFL Films. By the 1996 off-season, no fewer than five of the players Jones had once proudly hailed as being "in my image" were either on probation or under suspension by the league. It had reached the point where one Dallas sportswriter joked, "When the Cowboys go out to the center of the field before the game, they need two teams: one for the coin toss, the other to be read their Miranda rights."

And then, unbelievably, the 1997 season for Team Turmoil opened the same way the '96 one had ended. Only this time, in a take-off on the old Jimmy Durante line, "Everybody wants to get into the act," it wasn't one of the players, it was the coach, Barry Switzer. An old friend of Troy Aikman, long a non-fan of Switzer, left a message on Aikman's answering machine: "Guess what Dr. Einstein has done this time." What "Dr. Einstein," a.k.a. Switzer, had done was get himself arrested for carrying a loaded, unlicensed .38-caliber revolver in his carry-on luggage at the Dallas–Fort Worth Airport. This is the same Barry Switzer who had admonished his troops in the wake of their season-ending loss to Carolina in '96 to "be smart and make smart decisions." Even if, as someone suggested, anyone who coaches the Dallas Cowboys probably needs a loaded gun, his Stupid People Trick was enough to cause Cowboy watchers to wonder if Switzer, as they say down there, "could pour water out of a boot if the instructions weren't on the heel." Could the Cowboys' star be tarnished any more?

If the Cowboys are, as they claim, America's Team, then, as one Texan lamented, "Woe is America!"

STEVE BARTKOWSKI

HOW DO I HATE the Dallas Cowboys? Let me count the ways. . . .

1. They could have made the trade up from the number two spot in the 1975 NFL draft to the number-one position and picked me, rather than my being selected by the Atlanta Falcons.

2. They picked Randy White instead, and he terrorized me for my entire career.

3. They've *always* had all the luck—Hail Marys, comebacks, you name it—to win games over the years.

4. They're *always* on *Monday Night Football*.

5. They've got this attitude thinking they *are* America's Team.

———————

STEVE BARTKOWSKI was a quarterback for the Atlanta Falcons, Washington Redskins, and Los Angeles Rams from 1975 through 1986.

6. The people in Dallas actually think they're America's Team.

7. The referees always seem to favor them if there's any question on a judgment call or any gray area.

8. I hate Texas Stadium. . . . I mean, did they run out of money and couldn't afford to finish the roof?

9. They always have the best-looking cheerleaders.

10. They knocked me out of the playoffs two times.

Let's look at those ten reasons in, as they say, slo-mo.

Maybe some of my dislike for the Cowboys is shaped by the fact that back in 1975, when I was a senior at the University of California and eligible for the NFL draft that April, everyone had me slated as the number-one draft pick. The only question was: Which team?

The Baltimore Colts—remember them?—had the first draft choice by virtue of their having gone 2–12 in 1974. Second choice went to the Dallas Cowboys, less because of their 8–6 record, which kept them out of the playoffs for the first time in nine years, than because they owned the New York Giants' first draft choice. And the Atlanta Falcons were third, having come by their position honestly, their 1974 record, a woebegone 3–11.

Now, if you follow the NFL draft, you know that teams are always jockeying for position, trying to improve their spot in the draft by trading up to get a chance at selecting some particular player. The Colts were in the catbird's seat, owning that first selection. But they didn't need a quarterback since they already had a young up-and-coming one named Bert Jones.

Dallas was next in line and could have improved its position by trading up—swapping some player and the number-two pick or somesuch—to Baltimore for the number-one. The Cowboys had some real old guy at quarterback. I forget his name now, but I think he had gone to West Point or the Air Force Academy. . . . No, make that the Naval Academy . . . some guy named Roger Staubach. So they decided they'd sit tight with that number-two pick. And, as the fates would have it, the Atlanta Falcons were next.

Then, in one of the more brilliant predraft moves ever, the Falcons sent their best player, George Kunz—who just happened to be an offensive lineman—to Baltimore for the first pick, which they, in turn, used to select yours truly.

And the rest, as they say, is history. I ended up in Atlanta ducking blindside hits for three years because of some offensive lineman who wasn't there.

I've never really understood the rationale of building a team around a quarterback, as good as it sounds. It rarely works. Just ask me. Or Archie Manning or Jim Plunkett or Phil Simms or any other high first-round draft pick who ended up playing early on in his career with some really *bad* team. Only a few live to tell about their experiences. And even fewer have any football left in them by the time the building process is completed and they are surrounded, at long last, by some capable teammates.

So instead of being the number-two pick and learning at the knee of one of the true legends of the game, Roger Staubach, and then having him pass me the torch a few years down the road, I'm plunked smack-dab in the middle of a desperate situation, with little or no hope of seeing daylight—either figuratively or literally. It's somewhat like being adopted by a dysfunctional family: You just try to make the best of a tough situation.

Actually, I'm glad things worked out the way they did, because now, with a clear conscience, I can join the rest of the sane world in hating the Dallas Cowboys. Which is more fun and more fulfilling than any number of Super Bowl rings I would have won if I had been a member of the Cowboys.

And now, as an official member of the Cowboys-Haters Society of America, I can tell you that I'm sick and tired of seeing them on *Monday Night Football.* I mean, is there some broadcasting rule out there somewhere mandating that the Cowboys have to be on a nationally televised game at least every other week? Who makes up those schedules anyway? And just what formula do they use? The Cowboys have been forced down our throats more than broccoli down a five-year-old's by some network nitwits who probably are living out some childhood fantasy about riding the range with their six-shooters blazing away.

Attention, all network programming geeks: Give us a break! We're all sick and tired—or is that tired and sick?—of seeing *your* beloved Cowboys. Create some other media darling, some other version of America's Team, please! You've done it before; you can do it again. Maybe even the Atlanta Falcons, if you work hard enough at it.

In my estimation, the entire Cowboy TV ambience is more about midriffs and halter tops than about post patterns and draw plays. The one thing the Cowboy franchise has done—and very successfully, I might add—is develop and take cheerleading to (dare I say?) another level. Maybe this is why those network suits are so enamored with the Cowboys. Maybe it's not the Cowboys football team at all, but those dancing darlings down on the sidelines. After all, they're the real show. And worthy of their big reputation. Look at 'em; they're the best-looking of any group of cheerleaders in the NFL. Maybe even college football, too. It's gotten to the point where it seems as if a girl can't qualify for the cheerleading squad unless she has at least one Miss Texas title on her résumé.

The Dallas Cowboy Cheerleaders should have their own show. Why should they be a sideshow when they're the main event? Such a show would be a big hit, not only with Dallas fans but with all of us. And it would disassociate them from the team so many of us have come to love to hate. Just think of the new fan base: millions of fans who hate everything about the Cowboys, cheerleaders included. Now, with their own show, you could actually root for the cheerleaders without rooting for the Cowboys. And while we're at it, why not move them to another city, a city like Atlanta, where they could parade around on the Falcons' sidelines. It would be a perfect scenario because everybody, everywhere, loves Atlanta. Why not its cheerleaders, even if we had to adopt them from Dallas?

And what about that monstrosity called Texas Stadium? Did they just run out of money? Why, pray tell, didn't they put a roof on it? Is its purpose to provide cover for the fans but maintain the appearance of an open-air arena? If so, why not put natural grass there instead of that Stinkin' Astroturf? I'll bet whoever planned that never once thought of how all those shadows in the late afternoon would play havoc with their friends back at the television studios. It's the only stadium in the league where the phrase "run to daylight" still applies. As a fan, and as a TV viewer, you could be watching a handoff at midfield and then all of a sudden not be able to see the running back, who has disappeared breaking for the sidelines. You know what I'm talking about . . . you've seen the Shadows of Texas Stadium. It's almost like football's version of hide-and-seek.

And then there are the players. Always in trouble, the team always in turmoil. There have been so many travesties committed in the Cowboys' camp, I'm surprised that the Association of Professional Rodeo Cowboys (who, incidentally, are the *real* thing) hasn't petitioned the Cowboys to change their name. After all, if I'm a champion bullrider, I wouldn't want there to be any confusion between my bullriding and their bullshitting. Hey, in this age of political correctness, if Native Americans can get upset over the name Redskins, why can't *real* cowboys get equally upset about a group usurping and besmirching the name Cowboys?

And talking about the players, why is it that all Dallas players have their own TV and radio shows? Even a second-string defensive back has his own show, a show on which he talks about the strategies for the upcoming game and whatnot. How in the dickens does he know what strategies will be employed? All that he knows is what responsibility L-5 on the kickoff team has and what his personal responsibility is as the protector of the punter. Those are his only opportunities to step between the stripes on a Sunday afternoon. But here he is, speaking with all the authority of a Rush Limbaugh on politics every week. And with a far greater following.

Then there's the offensive player with his own TV show. In prime time, no less. Here's a guy who knows little or nothing about a comprehensive game plan, yet he rattles on about specific strategies for an hour or so.

The only comprehensive plan he's ever followed is the one he established to purchase contraband after the game.

How gullible can the Dallas Cowboys fan be if he listens to these clown-analysts? Who sponsors these shows anyway? Are they crazy?

Maybe it's just part of the overall climate in Dallas, where everybody—and I mean *everybody*—gets "community perks." Certainly there are two or three superstars on the Cowboys who deserve some "community perks"—meaning local endorsements, such as a car deal, a clothing deal, maybe even an endorsement for a local company or two. But in the Big D, *everybody* has a car deal.

When car deals and other local endorsements trickle down to the guy who rarely, if ever, plays, then something must be wrong. Are there that many car dealers in Dallas who can't get season tickets? Who have to swap a car for the player's "comps" (and here I use the word *player* very loosely)? Are tickets really that hard to come by? Is the dealer looking to sell more cars to a savvy buying public just because the left tackle on the punt team is driving one of *his* cars? Maybe this town is so backward that somehow he believes that he enhances his status by supplying cars to everyone but the assistant to the assistant towel carrier. Or just maybe it gives him something to brag about in his best Texas drawl at the next cocktail party—and that's how he gets his jollies down there in the Big D.

But the main reason I'm such a Cowboy-hater is that they knocked my Atlanta Falcons out of the playoffs. Not once, but twice. And shouldn't have. It was just that dumb, stupid "luck of the Cowboys."

The first time was in the 1978 playoffs. We were an

overachieving, upstart team with a great defense and an efficient offense, in the playoffs for the first time in our history. And here we were, a 9–7 team facing the 12–4 Cowboys. It was a dreary, miserable cold day in Dallas, and we almost pulled it off. Ahead 20–13 at halftime and with Roger Staubach out of the game with a concussion—wouldn't you know it?—Danny White comes in and somehow, some way, brings the Cowboys back, and they squeak out a 27–20 win.

And then there were the 1980 playoffs. That was the year Atlanta went 12–4 and won its first divisional title. We had the best team in the NFC, Dallas included—six Pro Bowlers on offense, a strong defense. We came out smoking and built a big lead, 24–10, after three quarters. We could have scored literally every time we had the ball. But Coach Leeman Bennett called off the dogs, and we went to our conservative "stall the ball" game, football's version of basketball's four-corner offense. And with Danny White pitching and Drew Pearson catching, they scored three times in the fourth quarter, the last time on a White-to-Pearson 23-yarder in the final minutes, to beat us. It was a real lollipop of a pass that defensive back Rolland Lawrence got turned around on and was beaten in the far corner of the north end zone.

Is it any wonder I hate the Dallas Cowboys?

SKIP BAYLESS

JUST FIVE YEARS AGO, the "New" Dallas Cowboys were America's darlings. They had risen from the 1–15 dead just three seasons earlier, and they had a fresh innocent cast of lovable underdogs. That team upset the 49ers in San Francisco and won its first Super Bowl.

How could the most avid Cowboys-hater find loathing in his or her heart for Troy or Emmitt or Michael or Jimmy?

But these "new" Cowboys, winners of three of the last five Super Bowls and five straight division titles, have grown obnoxiously old for many fans and media members around the country. That's certainly the feeling I get debating callers from coast to coast each week on ESPN Radio.

For decades, baseball's New York Yankees dominated the national sports psyche as the most/least popular team in sports. But even the Bronx Bombers never in-

---

SKIP BAYLESS, a former columnist for the Dallas Morning News *and the* Dallas Times Herald, *is a regular on ESPN's* Prime Monday *and* The Sports Reporters *and has written three books on the Cowboys*—God's Coach, The Boys, *and* Hell-Bent.

spired the degree of disgust the Cowboys have. And lately, it has been hard to hate the damn Yankees, who just won their first World Series in eighteen years.

Since the Cowboys' initial rise to power in the mid-1960s, they have been far more consistently embraceable *and* despicable than the Yankees, as witnessed by a recent Harris Poll survey, which found that while 21 percent of fans said the Cowboys are their favorite national team, 29 percent said the Cowboys are their least favorite.

At the risk of sounding even more presumptuous than the Cowboys are accused of being, let me say that no team has ever been more loved *and* hated than the current edition of the Cowboys.

This time around many fans in and out of Dallas seem turned off by much more than just the Cowboys' no-end-in-sight success. Michael Jordan's Chicago Bulls, who have won five of the last seven NBA titles, rival the Cowboys in popularity, but not unpopularity.

Here, with apologies to David Letterman, are ten reasons so many Americans now hate America's Team. . . .

10. The Texas-Sized Superiority Complex

The most detested Cowboys quality—arrogance—is more abundant than ever. If possible, these Cowboys are less humble than any of their famed predecessors. (What's next? A Cowboys book called *From Narcs to Narcissism*?) And they have spoiled their fans even more than Landry's teams did. They are never beaten by a better team or by an opponent that simply played better that day. No, these Cowboys can make excuses almost as fast as they can make big plays. They lose only because of Emmitt's sore hamstring or because Aikman can't throw a wet ball or because Irvin was suspended or triple-teamed. Cowboy fans around the country, taking their cue from their role-model stars, are probably the worst at gloating, at excuse-making—and at jumping quietly off the bandwagon when the Cowboys lose two in a row.

While the Redskins, Giants, and Eagles sell out season-ticket allotments no matter how sorry the team might be, Texas Stadium turned into a ghost town when it was no longer the place to be seen in 1988 and 1989. Yet when the Cowboys are winning, which is most of the time, most Cowboy-lovers consider themselves the world's best fans. Rival fans hate them for being so fickle, so elitist, so luxury-box . . . so Dallas.

9. Too Much of a Great Thing

Editors at sports magazines from L.A. to New York have a golden rule: When in doubt, put a Cowboy on the cover. Cowboys sell, they attract female as well as male readers simply because the Cowboys are the best soap opera in sports history—better than fiction; better than the TV soap opera *Dallas*. (What team has ever had a star receiver wind up the target of a foiled murder-for-hire plot involving a stripper and a police officer, like Michael Irvin?)

As Tex Schramm used to say, "The national media wants us to lose, but they don't want us to go away." And the sports magazine industry suffered greatly when the Cowboys became a 1–15 nonfactor.

Today it's impossible for a fan in any NFL city to go

into a grocery store without seeing Emmitt or Troy or Deion or—help!—Jerry, all part of the "Say Cheese" phenomenon, smiling from the magazine racks.

And though non-Cowboy fans will still read about the Cowboys, they're now finding the overexposure overbearing. Typical non-Cowboys fan: "I don't want to hear another word about the blankety-blank Dallas Cowboys. . . . What happened to Irvin today?"

8. The Designer Uniforms

When I meet Cowboy fans who live in other cities, they often tell me they were first attracted to the team because of the star on the sides of the Cowboys' helmets. Yet just as many non-Cowboys fans have told me they hate the Cowboys mostly because their metallic-blue uniforms are just too damned pretty. Too Gucci, too Armani. Football wasn't meant to be played in uniforms from Neiman-Marcus, they say. The uniforms remind them too much of Cowboys luxury-box fans, who dress for games as if they're at church. Which they are.

7. That Four-Letter Word Ending in U-C-K

The second most detested Cowboy quality—luck—is alive and well. And giving the NFL hell. Cowboy superstars almost never suffer season-ending or career-threatening injuries, and when they are hurt, the Cowboys can count on one-game wonders, like Clint Longley, to rescue their chestnuts from the fire.

Just when the world thinks it's safe to dance on the Cowboys' grave, a hand explodes up through the dirt—

or Astroturf—like the one at the end of *Carrie* and catches a Hail Mary, as Drew Pearson did a few years back in Minnesota to win a playoff game, or the team gets some other incredibly lucky break.

Yes, even with Jerry and Barry running the show, God still watches over His team through the hole in the Texas Stadium roof. Sickening, isn't it?

6. Troy Ache-Man

No matter how much the Cowboys win, Aikman always seems unhappy. He mopes. He whines. He's unsatisfied. He lashes out at bumbling teammates in full view of the cameras. He criticizes a head coach the rest of his teammates endorse. He bemoans the suspensions of the Irvins and Letts, saying, "The shine is off the [Cowboys'] star."

Informed Cowboy fans know that the hair-trigger perfectionist in Aikman is perhaps the biggest reason that he (and his team) have been so successful. But from a distance, Aikman comes across as Troy Angst-man, tormented by his miserable life. Non-Cowboy fans say, "If he thinks he has it so bad, he ought to try a season in Tampa Bay."

For non-Cowboy fans, Aikman doesn't quite have the redeeming qualities Roger Staubach had. Though Staubach didn't beat fans over the head with his faith, he made it clear that he was a Christian. Aikman is a snuff-dippin', beer-drinkin', pickup-drivin' country-music buff—a genuine cowboy who spent part of his childhood on a farm outside Henryetta, Oklahoma. Could any non-Cowboy fan truly hate Roger Staubach? Aikman is different.

5. "Emmy" Smith

After the Cowboys' final regular-season game of 1993 at Giants Stadium, John Madden made his first trip to a postgame locker room since becoming a TV commentator. He wanted to congratulate Emmitt Smith on "the most courageous performance [he'd] ever seen." The Cowboys had just won the NFC East by beating the Giants 16–13 in overtime. Emmitt had suffered a grade-two shoulder separation near the end of the first half but, dragging his arm like a broken wing, had run through the Giants time and again, finally breaking their will and their hearts.

Since then, Emmitt has turned into the star who cries wolf—or hamstring or knee or neck. Emmitt almost always seems to have something wrong with him. Yet Emmitt almost always plays. Especially when the Cowboys take the national stage on *Monday Night Football.*

Emmitt always seems to writhe on the ground after at least one play-ending whistle. Late in the Cowboys' 1996 season-opening, Monday-night loss in Chicago, Emmitt delayed the game for about ten minutes while he lay motionless after landing on his head. Could his career be ended by a spinal injury? Emmitt was rushed to the hospital, where he was kept overnight for tests. While doing a TV interview in a neck brace the next morning, Emmitt admitted that he could have walked off the field. He practiced the following day. He had experienced no more than a "stinger," a bolt of pain down the arm causing tingling or numbness in the hand. Many players routinely play through such stingers.

Is Emmitt's pain threshold courageously high or deceptively low? Before and during games, does he sometimes exaggerate the pain he feels to lull the opposition or to set himself up to win a Purple Heart? Does he love the constant media attention generated by the soap opera swirling around his almost weekly injuries? Emmitt's daily injury updates are more riveting than *General Hospital.*

Whatever, talk-show hosts outside Dallas are getting sick of "Emmy" Smith's act. I know, because during football season, I'm interviewed by five or six out-of-town shows each weekday. And I'm constantly bombarded with skeptical, sarcastic questions such as "Is Emmitt on his deathbed today? And do you figure he'll run for one hundred or two hundred yards on Sunday?"

Though Emmitt remains the most popular Cowboy nationally, many national media members wonder if the adoration is beginning to go to his helmet.

4. The Coach from Hell

Any football fan who admired—or feared—Tom Landry, "God's coach," surely detests Barry Switzer, who called his autobiography *Bootlegger's Boy.* From television, fans get two stunningly unimpressive views of Switzer: The first is of Switzer on the sidelines, looking bored or lost while listening via headphones to his coaches calling plays; the second is of Switzer in his press conferences, becoming unglued over routine questions and sometimes coming across more like an asylum escapee than the coach who now occupies Landry's old office.

Switzer tends to cuss in front of cameras, has been known to drink in public around Dallas, and occasionally visits topless clubs, furthering the national notion that he lets his Cowboys run wild and that they win in spite of this un-Landry. And many fans and journalists agree with Aikman, who has said, "I don't know what it is he does as head coach."

The truth is, Switzer's players (except for Aikman) love the coach because he's so genuine and has such big-hearted compassion for the physical battering they endure. Yet Cowboy-haters can't get over the perception that Jerry Jones hired this character only because he knew the grateful Switzer (who wouldn't have been hired by any other owner or college president) would become Jones's drinking-buddy puppet. Many fans believe that sooner or later, the Cowboys will be Barry-ed Alive.

3. Jerry!

No matter how successful Jerry Jones is—and judging purely by the results, he has proven to be one of the most successful owners in sports—many fans will never forgive him for (a) replacing Landry with Jimmy Johnson or (b) replacing Johnson with Barry Switzer. And no matter how desperately Jones wants to be loved, he always trips headlong over his camera-hogging ego.

To Jones's credit, highly respected journalists, such as Frank Deford of *Newsweek* and those at HBO's *Real Sports*, have often told me how much they appreciate his constant availability for interviews and his willingness to answer the toughest questions. Yet for Jones, the downside is that fans everywhere get sick of seeing his smiling mug on television. (He has the biggest eye-teeth this side of Transylvania.) Jerry in the owner's box; Jerry on the practice field; Jerry down on the sidelines during games. Jerry has become a more irritating national TV presence than the Energizer Bunny.

More and more, fans see Jones as an egomaniac who wants to be a bigger star than Troy or Emmitt.

On TV, as he continually tells America how "ever'thing's" just fine and dandy with his "Ca-boys," Jones comes across with all the sincerity of a phony televangelist or slippery politician—a real-life J. R. Ewing. Jones, in fact, sees J.R. as something of a role model. Jones is turning into the NFL's J.R.—the only-in-Dallas owner who has assembled the best team oil money could buy.

Though his ideas for improving the overall profits of NFL Properties make twenty-first-century sense, many fans see Jones as some sort of Grinch trying to steal the game of football by Jerry-rigging rules and hoarding league wealth and championships.

For many out-of-state fans, Jones represents everything they hate about the sometimes unjustified image of Dallas: coldhearted greed and soulless vanity. While former Cowboys president and general manager Texas E. Schramm was despised for his holier-than-thousands arrogance, Schramm was also respected for being a league loyalist with class and dignity. No such luck for Jerry-Jerry-quite-contrary.

2. Thirteen Million Dollars

Perhaps the biggest reason for the dramatic Harris Poll jump in Cowboy-haters—up a startling 14 percent from the previous Harris Poll—was the NFL-record $13 million bonus Jones paid to make Deion Sanders a Cowboy. Neon Deion is probably the most hated man in pro football (by the fans, not the players). When he was a 49er, Deion certainly was the most hated by Cowboy fans.

Though he clearly is the NFL's best athlete—and maybe the greatest cornerback who ever played—Deion is just about everything most male fans were taught not to be. He flaunts and he taunts. He goes into his showboating dance even before he reaches the goal line. He has inspired many of his Cowboy teammates to gyrate and celebrate after so much as making a first down. He refuses to get his uniform dirty unless absolutely necessary—only risking a high-speed collision to tackle a ballcarrier when he needs to save a touchdown.

Deion put Cowboy-haters over the top. He also helped put the Cowboys back on top.

1. The Midnight Cowboy(s)

Although no one really wants to hear—or remember—this, the Cowboys did *not* name themselves America's Team. NFL Films did. Yes, it's true that Tex Schramm had to approve the name given to the 1978 Cowboys' highlight film. And that he and his PR staff did nothing to discourage this pompous conceit. Still, it was the idea of NFL Films.

And yet, for reasons unknown, many Americans seem to believe that with the title America's Team went the responsibility of being America's foremost role models. Holy Cowboy! Because of the temptations and idolatry in Dallas, the Cowboys have always made the worst role models of any team in any city.

Still, when Michael Irvin was caught in a motel room with drugs and topless dancers, it was as if some Jimmy Swaggart or Jim Bakker had been exposed; as if a role-model Cowboy had been living a lie. For Irvin, this was fairly routine after-hours behavior. But, as he joined substance abusers Leon Lett, Clayton Holmes, and Shante Carver on the NFL's suspended list, fans everywhere condemned the Cowboys as two-faced hypocrites.

True, but crazy and unfair.

As Landry once said, "I think that 'America's Team' title gave us a lot more trouble than it was worth."

As long as Landry was coaching, Cowboy cheerleaders flashing a little T&A was okay for the most pristine fans. It was like justifying buying *Playboy* for the in-depth interviews. But after the Irvin trial's strip-and-tell testimony, the Cowboys' image went from barely-in-bounds *Playboy* to out-of-bounds *Hustler*. You could hear ideals shattering all over America.

Maybe the Cowboys aren't so lovable anymore, but what Cowboy-hater wouldn't trade teams with Dallas?

GREG BUTTLE

THE DALLAS COWBOYS, AMERICA'S Team? What gall! What hubris! What bullshit!

For any team—let alone the Dallas Cowboys—to wrap themselves in a patriotic banner, demanding that we regard them as America's Team would piss off a Good Humor man. It certainly does most Americans and almost every player on every other team in the NFL when they hear that phrase.

To call Dallas America's Team is about as absurd and as far-fetched as the belief that Americans would want *their* team represented by drug dealers, criminals, con men, and other lowlifes, or that the same motley contingent who stay at the Cowboys' party house, known as "the White House," could be overnight guests at *the* White House at 1600 Pennsylvania Avenue. Wait a minute... that's not as far-fetched as I thought.

Let's step back a second to consider what those two overwrought words, *America* and *Americanism*, which have somehow, some way, lost their meaning in mod-

---

GREG BUTTLE was a linebacker on the New York Jets from 1976 through 1984.

ern society, really mean—especially in light of the Cowboys having taken the liberty of calling themselves America's Team.

As Theodore Roosevelt—you remember him, don't you? (no, like almost all great Americans, he never played for America's Team)—once said, and I certainly agree, "Americanism is a question of principle, of idealism, of character; it is not a matter of birthplace, creed, or line of descent." Nor, might I add, what team one plays for.

Over the years, I've found that Americans play to win, not to tie or come in second but to win, period. And whether it is winning on the NFL gridiron or in the arena of Presidential politics, the object of the game is to win. Or in the immortal words of Al Davis, "Just win, baby!" Or maybe that was Bill Clinton. Either way, you get the idea.

Want to win? Then pile it on, take no prisoners, punish the wounded, and let nothing stop you in the name of victory. You want to win the Super Bowl? Want to win the Presidency? Same thing.

Americans are blindly driven to do whatever is necessary for that victory, to do whatever it takes to get the job done. Hold your opponents, leg-whip 'em, kick 'em in the balls, and when they're down, do it again so they can't get up. Then deny you did it and say something to the effect of "But everybody else is doing it, and I promise I won't do it again." And then when you get away with it, do it again and again and again. . . . Anything goes when the name of the game is "win," whether in football or politics.

And why do most Americans appreciate this kind of behavior? Because you're a winner, and most Americans love a winner—just ask the Dallas Cowboys.

I'm sorry, but I can't agree with that type of thinking. And here I refer again to Theodore Roosevelt: "Americanism is a question of principle, of idealism, of character. . . ." And principle, idealism, and character mean a helluva lot more than just winning one Super Bowl or one election.

That's why, even though the Dallas Cowboys think they've cornered the market on Americanism by loudly proclaiming themselves to be America's Team, they will never ever truly be America's Team. Their win-at-any-cost philosophy is one that no American who shares the values this country was built on can identify with.

No, the Dallas Cowboys, if they are anything, are the Anti-America's Team, a team that exhibits none of the virtues associated with Americanism. They have none of the principle, idealism, or character that go with being America's Team.

I'm sure I join every right-thinking football fan when I say that I detest America's Team and what they stand for—even though I must confess I have always liked Roger Staubach and Tom Rafferty, but then again, they are the Cowboys of yesteryear.

It's time for the Cowboys to either clean up their act or abdicate their title. They're no more America's Team than our White House mob, although they do possess some of the same traits.

BILL CONLIN

PHILADELPHIANS HATE DALLAS IN the springtime, when it drizzles. We hate Dallas in the summer, when it sizzles. We hate Dallas in the winter, when it freezes. And above all, Philly hates Dallas in the fall, when the football team breezes. Oh, Jesus!

How do we hate the Dallas Cowboys? Let me count the ways. And the hatred that people of the Philadelphia persuasion—most of them bleak-outlooking, blue-collar nihilists—have locked in their hearts is much more complex than that of, say, Metroplex postal workers. I have heard that deep in the bowels of the main post office in Dallas—not far from Lee Harvey Oswald's last, gut-clutching stand—there is a therapy room for postal employees who feel they are ready to do the McDonald's thing. Or hijack a school bus.

I hear there is a wall filled with Dallas Cowboy mug shots.

Uptight certified-letter clerks and harassed operators of the constantly jamming sorting machines may check

---

BILL CONLIN has been a columnist for the Philadelphia Daily News *since 1965 and a panelist on ESPN's* Sports Reporter *since 1988.*

out a paintball-firing automatic weapon and blaze away. Whoever can put the tightest pattern on Michael Irvin wins a free weekend with one of the wideout's covey of self-employed models.

In Philadelphia, we have more creative therapy. The throwing-snowballs-at-Santa-Claus thing has been vastly overrated. Actually, on that almost forgotten day in Franklin Field, the jolly old elf had been commissioned to circle the track at halftime and peg miniature footballs into the stands. Some of the footballs contained choice tickets to the next season's games. Alas, St. Nick had an arm like a Phillies outfielder. And when his attempts to reach the Franklin Field upper deck fell far short, the drunken denizens seated there let loose with a furious salvo of frozen missiles made possible by a recent snowstorm.

It was nothing personal. Just business, as they say in the barber shops, pizza parlors, and cheesesteak emporiums of South Philly.

The folks who threw snowballs at Santa represent the sunny side of Philadelphia's outer self—the smiling, generous child in us. They are the grinning free spirits who say, "Yo . . . Michael Irvin and Jerry Jones are sitting on the bench in preseason at The Ranch. Two Dallas Cowboys cheerleaders walk by on their way to practice. Irvin nudges his owner. 'Wanna fuck 'em?' he asks. Jerry Jones replies, 'Out of what?' "

On the flip side of that good-natured bonhomie is Ben Franklin's evil twin. It seems that for every Marian Anderson, Stan Getz, and Rocky Balboa we produce; Philly also breeds a Gary Heidnick, the Duncan Hines of cannibalistic serial killers.

And the most egregious example of this dark side came on a bright May day in 1985, when Philadelphia made a perverse kind of military history. In 1812 British men-of-war bombarded Fort McHenry, a minor military annoyance, with the unhappy side effect of inspiring Baltimore's Francis Scott Key to compose an anthem that invites the kind of pregame mutilation it deserves and almost always receives.

That was one bombing of American soil.

In 1941 a Japanese submarine surfaced and lobbed a few harmless shells at a coastal oil refinery in Southern California. Uncle Sam responded to this miniscule annoyance by herding hundreds of thousands of Japanese Americans into concentration camps, where most of them languished four long years. Hollywood committed an even more heinous crime: It made the John Belushi movie titled *1941*.

That made two bombings of American soil.

But until May of 1985, no American city had been bombed from the air. Certainly, no American city had been bombed by its own police department.

So listen up, Dallas Cowboys fans, this will give you just a little better feel for what we're all about than does snowballing Santa or booing unwed mothers on Mother's Day. It speaks more to our "Fire up the *Enola Gay*" toughness than does booing orphans who fail to find an egg in the Easter egg hunt, or even the way we practice booing, which is to stand on a bridge over the Schuylkill River and boo also-rans in the Dad Vail Regatta.

When a long confrontation between police and a back-to-nature cult called MOVE escalated into gunfire, the Philadelphia Air Force roared into action. A police helicopter dropped what was euphemistically called "an explosive device" on the roof of the MOVE row house. A bomb! Hundreds of gallons of fuel were stored in containers there to run the cult's generators, the city having long since cut off the utilities.

The MOVE members were pinned in the cellar by intense police sniper fire. The flames moved faster than Citizen Jones when he fired Tom Landry and Tex Schramm. A dozen cult members died and fifty-six row houses—an entire city block—went up in a raging conflagration.

So . . . Now that you know who you're fucking with, Cowboys, let's turn to football.

Six months before the MOVE incident the Cowboys flogged the Eagles 34–17, starting a four-game losing streak that knocked them out of playoff contention. Before that grim season began, the Eagles were all but in Phoenix, as cash-strapped owner Leonard Tose fought an unsuccessful rearguard action against the banks that held the notes on the team. Then former Philadelphian and current Miami luxury auto dealer Norman Braman rode to the rescue. Before the final game of the 1985 season, Braman fired Marion Campbell. And when he failed to hire young David Shula, son of Don, Braman hired crusty, irascible Bears defensive specialist Buddy Ryan. He was the architect of the vastly overrated "46" defense that worked so well when manned by All-Pros from a Super Bowl defense.

Before Buddy, true hatred for the Cowboys was more regional and historical than based on any particular incidents. In fact, Philadelphia fans were split into two factions when Ryan came along. Fans who remembered Pearl Harbor were old enough to appreciate the brilliance of the Eagles teams that won NFL titles in 1948 and 1949 after losing the title game in 1947. That seminal era finally came to an end in 1960, when the Eagles beat Vince Lombardi's Green Bay Packers on the Jell-O pudding gridiron of Franklin Field.

As Buddy Ryan began his blustering career with a braying radio show on a new all-sports radio station,

WIP, the graybeards were opposed by a new breed of "passionate" follower, to borrow a talk-radio buzzword. These people were destined to be the infantry in the one-way but bitter trench warfare against the hated Cowboys. They wore the ugly green apparel that the NFL had begun to market, tailgated relentlessly, and either puked or peed in every cranny of befouled Veterans Stadium.

And as the creativity of their delinquency matured, they would pelt the reviled Jimmy Johnson—not Santa Claus—with lethal iceballs, not fluffy snowballs.

Buddy Ryan's disdain for the enemy orchestrated their peevish ire just as surely as Eugene Ormandy's baton pulled soaring crescendos from the string section of the Philadelphia Orchestra.

For this younger, harder-drinking, decidedly blue-collar season ticket holder, there was no NFL before Super Bowl I. Nothing happened until the Voice of God, ubiquitous Philadelphia TV news personality John Facenda, turned the "frozen tundra" of Green Bay into a religious shrine. And looking at their beloved "Iggles" through that flawed prism, they agreed that the Eagles' modern era began on the great, getting-up afternoon of January 11, 1981.

Lined up on the other side of the ball on the Eagles' first possession of the NFC title game on a brutally cold 20-degree day were Landry's lordly Cowboys. They were favored to win the game even though the Eagles won the division and had the home field advantage throughout the playoffs. But Wilbert Montgomery, the Birds' popular workhorse, slashed through a gaping hole, cut back, and raced untouched for a long touchdown. The air rushed out of the benumbed Cowboys, who collapsed like an overbaked soufflé. The 20–7 victory took the Eagles to the Super Bowl. Few remember the flat effort that caused them to be gangplanked in New Orleans by the wild-card Oakland Raiders.

When today's character-assassinating WIP hosts ask callers to name Philadelphia's all-time sports moment, the inevitable winner, cleats down, is Wilbert Montgomery's run in a penultimate game.

That it happened against the Dallas Cowboys has come to mean everything.

By 1986 Landry's Cowboys were deep into their Decline and Fall of the Roman Empire imitation. Buddy Ryan split with the Fervent Fedora. Same result in 1987, but with a huge difference. . . .

There was the bitter players' strike. In Philly, Ryan remained loyal to his picketing players and treated the scabs like, uh, scabs. In Dallas, Landry signed the best replacement team available, looking for an edge. His strikebreakers flogged Ryan's brutally bad pseudo-Iggles, 44–21.

The luck of the schedule had the Eagles and Cowboys playing again the first Sunday after the strike ended. With the game safely won and nothing more required of quarterback Randall Cunningham than to take a knee, Buddy orchestrated this: Cunningham faked taking a knee, sprang up, and threw a touchdown pass for a 37–20 victory.

That began an unprecedented run of Eagles victories over the Cowboys, who did not bottom out until Jimmy Johnson's 1–15 debut. Philadelphia beat the 'Pokes 24–23, 23–7, 27–0, 20–10, 21–20, 17–3, and 24–0. Ryan had been replaced by Rich Kotite in 1991. The highlight of his 24–0 victory were nine—count 'em—sacks of rookie coach Jimmy Johnson's quarterback, Troy Aikman.

In the 700 level of Veterans Stadium, life was good. The

polyester green jackets felt like imported silk, the beer tasted like Dom Perignon, and the hoagies could have been croissants filled with wafer-thin carpaccio and brie.

And this became the new problem. As the Eagles' fortunes under Kotite slowly eroded and Johnson began leading the Cowboys to Super Bowls, the fans expected—no, demanded—Dallas to hate them back.

They thought the first thing that fans of America's Team did in the week leading up to an Eagles game was wake up and immediately reach for the phone to call Norm Hitzges and rip the hated Eagles. Instead, Cowboy fans reached for what they usually reached for. Then they smoked a cigarette and breakfasted on yogurt and Raisin Bran.

To this day it infuriates Iggles fans that no matter how hard they hate the Cowboys, their demented dudgeon is simply not shared in the town where, on a clear day, you can see the flames from the Branch Davidian's complex in Waco.

Philadelphians, so proud of their colonial heritage, Quaker thrift, and record of having lost more baseball games than any major league city in history, came up empty on the anorexic history of Dallas, Fort Worth, and Irving—named for 1897 deli owner Irving Crockett.

Were it not for the invention of air-conditioning, Dallas would have remained a dusty rail hub for the transport of cattle, a place for ranchers to sow their wild oats, barley, and other more nutritious seed at the kind of watering hole Jack Ruby was running when he avenged Jack.

Modern Dallas was settled by outsiders with clean fingernails. The image-conscious football team put together by Schramm and Landry, with help from a computer-pioneering personnel director named Gil Brandt, was perfect for a population on the move. They even needed the paradox of the pious Landry juxtaposed against the bawdy image set forth by former Cowboy wideout Peter Gent in *North Dallas Forty.* The real Cowboys were a lot closer to the transgressions of a wide range of sinners and the porn classic *Debbie Does Dallas.* Before Michael Irvin and Erik Williams, there were Lance Rentzel and Hollywood Henderson. And many, many others.

The hate of Iggles fans for their Cowboys counterparts has never been reciprocated. When the Iggles were enjoying their modest run of success under Buddy Ryan, the Cowboys were in a protracted down cycle. Everybody was whupping up on them. It is not as if Philadelphia was performing some great football feat.

Then when Jimmy Johnson turned it around, the Eagles were heading south under Rich Kotite.

WIP's mavens of misery keep flogging the dead horse, however. There is a morning drive-time zombie named Angelo Cataldi, a sterile Howard Stern who was once a solid football writer for the *Philadelphia Inquirer* before WIP part-owner and former Eagles great Tom Brookshier pointed him toward his $500,000-a-year destiny.

Twice more this year, and, hopefully, for the sake of the nineteen-to-forty-five male demographics, a third time in the playoffs, Cataldi and the spear-carriers who follow him through the day will fan the fires of hatred for America's Team. On a weekly TV panel show he moderates, Cataldi, who combines the gauntness of Ichabod Crane and the schnozz of Cyrano de Bergerac, will whip his T-shirted and green-jacketed audience to a frenzy, using all the communications skills that go with a master's degree from the Columbia School of Journalism.

In Dallas, however, where they killed our President with a magic bullet, the fans look beyond the Eagles. Or look back, depending on the schedule. What concerns real Cowboys fans is not the dog-ass, canned-beer-swilling, cholesterol-mainlining, ugly-woman-marrying Iggles fans who keep calling Norm during the week.

No, it is the Washington Redskins that matter in Dallas. The Redskins and the annual game where they whip the Green Bay Packers' butts. Even the Giants are bigger than the ho-hum Eagles.

How 'bout them Iggles? Just more lumps of reeking roadkill on the freeway to Texas Stadium.

CHET COPPOCK

CHICAGO IS MY KINDA town. A stand-up town, Old Man Daly's town. And even though his son, Richie, occupies the mayor's chair and prides himself on planting trees, a legit Chicagoan knows that the aura of Richard M. Daly is still the boldfaced personality of the city by Lake Michigan.

Chicagoans also understand the magnificence of Michigan Avenue, the sunshine magic of a summer cruise on Lake Shore Drive. Lincoln Park, River North, chic and hip. But in Chicago you look to the old-fashioned neighborhoods: the Italians on Taylor Street, the Poles on the Northwest Side, the elderly Jews who refuse to budge from Rogers Park. And they all endure, laughing at the biting chill that sweeps off the Lake during the winter months.

Chicago is a city with a big-time heart, a city with a degree of defiance. The collars are primarily blue. You want to play ball in the Windy City, you get a union card, you earn a check, you follow in your old man's footsteps.

CHET COPPOCK is a nationally known host on Sports-Channel and has served as the Chicago Bears' public-address announcer for eight seasons.

And you don't ask for a free ride. (That is, unless you've got a "Chinaman," which is Chicagoese for a friend at City Hall who can get you lined up with a city job in return for your pulling the lever once—maybe twice or three times—for every candidate who carries the colors of the Democratic Party.)

Sure, it's Capone's town. Always was; always will be. And an alderman isn't really considered to be on the square unless he's been connected with at least a couple of phony land deals.

But, above all, it's George Halas's town. George Halas, a local boy made good, a Chicago bohunk. George Halas, Papa Bear. George Halas, pro football's godfather. George Halas, the guy who moved pro football from the back of the paper, underneath the shipping news, to the front page by signing Harold "Red" Grange to a contract back in 1925 in a move that kept pro football in business.

Do you honestly think that Cowboys owner Jerry Jones can relate to what Halas went through during the Depression years? Jones never had to scurry to the box office on game day to get his mitts on the first slice of available cash and then zip over to the nearby pharmacy to buy tape for his players' ankles.

I doubt if Jones can even spell the word *tradition.* Or if he ever heard of Jim Thorpe's Indians or the Portsmouth Spartans. Can Jerry even spell the name Curly Lambeau?

Bill Gleason, the Chicago sports guru who began covering sports back when Sid Luckman was a teenager, said, "It would have been very difficult for Jerry Jones to get into the league if George Halas had been sitting on the executive council. But we also have to deal with the present. Money speaks."

And it spoke loud in Jerry Jones's case, with his ponying up untold millions to claim ownership of America's Team. And take his place at the NFL table.

What kind of man is Jones? Skip Bayless, a superb journalist who has written three best-sellers on the Cowboys, insists that J. R. Ewing, the blood-and-guts character who made the TV series *Dallas* a twenty-four-karat-gold hit, was Jerry Jones before Jerry Jones came up with the cabbage to buy the 'Boys. "Actually, J.R. is Jerry's role model or hero," Bayless says. "J.R. stands for what a lot of Dallas people stand for: They're arrogant, ruthless businessmen and very successful."

And if you think about it, it's a natural. J.R. was always trying to screw his family. Jones has seen him and raised him one, trying to screw his extended family, the National Football League. Jones figures that if you sign Deion Sanders and embarrass the NFL and your fellow owners, if you sell your soul to Nike and hop into bed with Pepsi-Cola, then you have qualified for Big D sainthood. On second thought, Jones probably bought the Cowboys because he thought it might get him better seats at SMU home games.

But Jones and Dallas are a perfect fit. What, exactly, does Dallas have? "There is no lake, no waterway, no sound, no water of any kind," says Bayless of Dallas. "There really is no reason for Dallas to exist. There's no Disney World or Bourbon Street. There's no beauty to Dallas. I've always said, 'It's a nice place to live, but you wouldn't want to visit there.' "

Chicago has its Rush Street and nightlife. Dallas? You talk about chicken-fried boredom: The streets are locked up at 4:00 P.M., and the Texas two-step is still all the rage.

Doug Buffone, who spent fourteen years playing for the Bears and is now a Chicago-based broadcaster, says, thinking of the Cowboys, "I wanted them to be like the guys on the Ponderosa. You know—big, friendly guys. In Dallas you thought of someone riding around in a Cadillac with a big-steer horse on the front going 'Ooga-Ooga.' "

Be honest now, how many cities can you name where your social status is measured by having a big-steer horse on the front going "Ooga-Ooga"? Or by the texture of your lizard-skin cowboy boots? I mean, Chicago can give you the St. Valentine's Day Massacre, Dillinger meeting his maker outside the historic Biograph Theatre, even Jackie "the Lackie" Cerone. The best Dallas can come up with is Michael Irvin pretending he's auditioning for a remake of *Superfly* and the Cowboys' social retreat, their so-called White House, where Cowboy players reenact their version of *Debbie Does Dallas.*

Jay Mariotti, the take-no-prisoners columnist for the *Chicago Sun-Times,* has his own take on what Dallas is all about. "It's the damnedest thing I've ever seen," Mariotti says, remembering his visit to the Big D a few years back. "I was there on a Sunday night after a playoff game, and Jerry Jones had his own show. So did Michael Irvin and a couple of other guys. It was completely out of control. I remember Randy Galloway from the *Dallas Morning News* had Nate Newton on his show. They're talking football and all of a sudden Galloway looks into the camera and says, 'All right, ladies and gentlemen, straight from Austin, Texas, the Shitkickers' (or whatever they were called), and Galloway is clapping like it's a variety show. I thought, What's going on here? This place is absolute lunacy. I guess that's what Dallas is in a nutshell."

Maybe that's why Dallas has embraced the Cowboys. It's *all* they have. They're an image, a feeding, an ego boost for a city that suffers from a horrible lack of self-esteem. But America's Team?

"The Dallas Cowboys never were America's Team," says Bill Gleason. "They weren't Chicago's team. And if you're not Chicago's team, you can't be America's Team!"

Gleason has a valid point. For Chicago has fielded the likes of Bronko Nagurski, Mean Ed Sprinkle, George Trafton, Bulldog Turner, Dick Butkus, and Mike Ditka—all symbols of America's toughness. Ditka especially was the ideal Bear. Blessed with the temper of a pit bull, he was the pupil who carried on the Halas tradition of "bust their jaws first, ask questions later." A brilliant tight end for the Bears during the 1960s, Ditka jumped the Bears' ship, telling everyone within earshot who would listen that Halas "tossed nickels around like manhole covers." That didn't prevent a forgiving Papa Bear from bringing Ditka back into the fold—not incidentally, from Dallas, where he had been working as a special-teams coach under Tom Landry and doing little more than establishing league records for throwing clipboards.

And the Dallas Cowboys? What players have worn their silver-and-blue to justify their claim to being America's Team? Deion Sanders? Michael Irvin?

Sanders is an example of the kind of Cowboy you could learn to dislike in . . . oh . . . fifteen to twenty seconds. "I don't think you have to worry about his breaking his shoulder pads or helmet," volunteers Dan Hampton, former Chicago Bears defensive lineman and future Hall of Famer. Deion's *mano a mano* style of play calls for him to play sixty minutes and completely avoid physical contact, all the better to live another day so that he can sign at least another half a dozen multimillion-dollar endorsement deals. Chuck Bednarik, a player in the great Chicago tradition even though he played for the Eagles, and the last great two-way player, saw more contact in a week than Sanders will see if he plays sixteen years. No, the Sanders persona is one made on Madison Avenue and Rodeo Drive, not on the gridiron.

And then there's Michael Irvin. Dan Hampton figures that Irvin's motel escapade with those two young Dallas debutantes was nothing more than par for the Cowboy course. He knows the Cowboy approach to such problems: " 'This guy [Irvin] went off the road. Let's get him back on it as fast as we can. We don't want to worry about any damage.' It's an attitude that's permeated that club for many years. A lot of people get special treatment, and they're thankful for it. The Cowboys expect it. They think that winning games transcends the norms of values and cultures, so they don't have to adhere to the rules like everyday people," says the Danimal.

But that's only Deion and Michael. What about the rest of the Cowboys and their image as America's Team? Here we again call on Bill Gleason. " 'America's Team' was strictly a catchphrase. There never has been an America's Team. When the New York Yankees had their great run of success, people all over the country hated them. The unfortunate thing is that the Cowboys, who've had great success in recent years, have become a burlesque of themselves; a parody. They're ridiculous!"

Doug Buffone seconds the emotion, hating both the Cowboys and their image. "It probably goes back to naming yourself America's Team. They look at you as if they're a Mercedes and you're a Yugo. At times, I liked that attitude. But it kept getting bigger."

Re-enter Bayless for a curtain call: "If you want to look at the Cowboys as role models, it's just one big hoot. To me, that's laughable because they've never been anything close."

We can tick off, in addition to Irvin, the names of Hollywood Henderson, Golden Richards, Lance Rentzel, Harvey Martin, and Duane Thomas. If that's America's Team, why don't they just drop the New York Giants from their schedule and add Leavenworth? Alcatraz would fit in nicely for an old-timers' game.

Oh, that image of America's Team. If you aren't sick of hearing that nonsense, you should be. Or else you're the kind of person who can hardly wait to purchase an official Deion Sanders "doo" rag. Let's at least pray for the continuation of the Dallas Cowboy Cheerleaders. Lose the gals, lose the hot pants, lose the cleavage, and you eliminate the word *bimbo* from twentieth-century jargon.

America's Team? I have the feeling that John Wayne was meant to be a Bears fan while Hugh Grant and Divine Brown would fit in nicely with the quiche eaters in the Texas Stadium sky suites.

DAVID DAVIS

YOU CAN'T SPELL HATE without *hat,* and I always hated the hat. In fact, my hatred for the Dallas Cowboys begins with the hat.

Tom Landry's hat, that is. The one you always saw crisply perched atop Landry's skull, seemingly in formation with his granite jaw. It was a conservative fedora—a distant cousin of the models that Paul "Bear" Bryant and Vince Lombardi sported in, respectively, Alabama and Wisconsin—and it moved up and down the sidelines like a small periscope coursing through the water, always focused on the action.

The hat was an extension of Landry's persona, and you could tell by looking at him that everything was just so in his life. Neat, stoic, utilitarian. Like how he got the Cowboys' offensive line to move together into position. Roger Staubach (later, Danny White) would come up to the line of scrimmage, settle over the center, and yell out something. The linemen would then do this upward hitch movement in rhythm before settling into their

---

DAVID DAVIS is the sports editor of the L.A. Weekly *and has had his efforts included in the annual anthology* Best American Sports Writing.

crouches in perfect synchronicity. No other team did this; quite frankly, I don't think most O-linemen could handle the dual chores of elaborate choreography and remembering the play. You'd see those grunts stagger up to the line, arrange themselves in something that vaguely resembled a row, and gamely lower themselves into a crouch. Not Cowboy material.

To me, the Dallas Cowboys were an extension of Landry's personality, which was why I began first to dislike them mildly and then to actively root against them. The Cowboys represented order and stability, and their strategy was all about winning performance. They ran complex defensive formations called the Flex, and they revived the Shotgun. Off the field, media types referred to them as "the Dallas Cowboys organization," as if they were a corporate entity rather than a football team. And, in a sense, they were. Long before current owner Jerry Jones snuggled up to Nike, the Cowboys symbolized the coming corporatization of football. As the IBM of professional sports, the Cowboys' innovations included their own unique (and very successful) scouting operation, which employed a "computer evaluation system," "personality questionnaires," and timed 40-yard dashes. The days of watching game film became obsolete, pronto.

Despite the technological imagery that accompanied the team, their superstars (Staubach, Tony Dorsett, Randy White, et al.) were always portrayed as selfless humanitarians. I cringed whenever those sappy United Way ads came on the TV on Sunday afternoons. The commercials always seemed to feature a Cowboy dressed in a plaid shirt, Lee jeans, and a corduroy blazer, sitting in front of a fireplace (was a fireplace really necessary in Dallas?) with a blond wife and seven blond kids, speaking slowly in a deep Dallas drawl as he struggled to balance a baby on one knee and to read the script some P.A. was holding up off-camera.

"Hi—my wife Wynette and I are lucky. We have seven healthy kids. But others aren't so fortunate." (Shot of Cowboy and wife visiting with a sick-looking child in a hospital bed.) "Won't you help others in need? Give to the United Way." (Music swells as we return to the living-room shot and the family's dog comes into the picture, panting at the heat from the fireplace.)

The saccharine aftertaste of the Cowboys was just too thick to take. Even the one aspect of the franchise that should have excited me—the vaunted Dallas Cowboys cheerleading squad and their lurid display of T&A—was an absurdity. Granted, these women were beautiful. But they dressed up in the most vampish outfits, with tight hot pants, calf-high white go-go boots like the type Nancy Sinatra used for "These Boots Were Made for Walking," and halter tops. This was pure schmaltz—a blow-dried version of American Dream women. That is, if your dreams were for the Mae West, Vegas showgirl look.

The Cowboys came off as, well, orchestrated. As fake as the breast implants some of the cheerleaders had. And during the late 1960s and early 1970s, this was exactly the opposite of what my friends and I wanted our heroes to be about. In the Age of Aquarius, Vietnam, and Watergate, when young people like my friends and I distrusted authority and preferred our heroes to be flawed, grizzly, and very real, that meant people like Joe Namath, Muhammad Ali, Jimi Hendrix. They were quintessentially American by being anti-establishment.

Not so the Cowboys. For many weekend-warrior fans— the Joe Six-Packs whose Sundays were spent worshiping at the pulpit of the end zone—the Cowboys took the fun out of the game. Dallas wasn't a real team; they were "a well-oiled machine." They didn't have personality like the Washington Redskins offensive linemen known as "the Hogs." Nor were they as gnarly as the outlaw Oakland Raiders, whose fans painted themselves in silver-and-black pirate outfits and beat up opposing teams' fans. The most radical thing the Cowboys had going for them was the hole in the roof of their stadium, for God's sake.

Dallas also refused to apologize for any of this. Instead, they wrapped themselves in the traditional values of America, an image reinforced by the fact that the Cowboys annually played on Thanksgiving Day. Who in the NFL okayed this deal—my guess is that the off-season visits by the cheerleading squad to the NFL's New York offices was the deal-clincher—and ruined our national holiday? I mean, it's bad enough that we have to hear Uncle Al go on about his goiter surgery for three hours at the dinner table. But to also have to watch the Cowboys play—and invariably win—was a double-dose of Thanksgiving evilness. (No wonder so many people die over this holiday weekend.)

My resentment boiled over when the media began to foist the label "America's Team" on the Cowboys. According to a book called the *Dallas Cowboys Encyclopedia,* this practice was started by the NFL Films' Bob Ryan in 1978. I don't remember a national referendum taking place to determine this, but I can tell you that my friends and I began to openly hate the Dallas Cowboys from that point on. My America was not the Dallas Cowboys, and the Dallas Cowboys were not my heroes.

This hiding-behind-the-flag wasn't the only element that I resented about the Cowboys. Another was their phenomenal on-field success. Call it the New York Yankee affliction. Or the Boston Celtics syndrome. But I naturally sided with the underdog, and being from New York, I sided with the New York Giants. (Or as broadcaster Marty Glickman used to call them, "the New York football Giants," as if an entity called "the New York baseball Giants" still existed in the 1970s.) During the brutal hiatus between, roughly, the departure of Frank Gifford and the coming of Bill Parcells, the Giants were dominated by the Cowboys, often twice a year. From 1964 to 1987, the Cowboys' regular-season record over the Giants was 34–7–1.

Why the Cowboys won so often was a no-brainer: Their personnel was consistently better than every other team's. Think of their many Pro Bowl players, guys like Bob Lilly, Mel Renfro, Lee Roy Jordan, Cliff Harris, Charlie Waters, "Too Tall" Jones, Harvey Martin, Troy Aikman, and on and on. It was no wonder that they made it to eight Super Bowl appearances, with five Super Bowl wins. For a while there, it was like they had a lock on talent.

Actually, despite their success, it wouldn't have taken much for Dallas to let us into the family. If the Cowboys had winked at us—if they had let us know that they didn't take themselves and the shotgun and their cheerleaders so damn seriously—it might have been okay. At the very least, we would've admired their winning ways. But the Cowboys refused to apologize for themselves, and that's why when the luster began to fade from the organization, when all the off-field transgressions began to outnumber the Super Bowl appearances, the sympathy was nonexistent.

The list is a long one, but you'd probably have to start with Lance Rentzel. Traded by the Vikings to the Cowboys in 1967 after a disorderly conduct conviction, Rentzel became a star receiver for Dallas, even leading the team in receptions for three years. He seemed to have it all—including a marriage to actress Joey Heatherton—but a few days before the 1970 Thanksgiving Day game, Rentzel was charged with indecent exposure to a minor. He pled guilty and quit the team; eventually, he was traded to the Rams.

Then there was Thomas "Hollywood" Henderson, a linebacker who gained fame at the 1978 Super Bowl with his classic line "[Pittsburgh Steelers quarterback] Terry Bradshaw couldn't spell *cat* if you spotted him the *c* and *t*." Long after Bradshaw had picked apart the Cowboys in the Steelers' 35–31 win, Henderson would admit to heavy cocaine use during his career. (Thankfully, Bradshaw never challenged Henderson to spell *coke*.)

More? Here's a partial update: Rafael Septien was the Cowboys' place-kicking specialist who set all sorts of team scoring records during his eight-year career. After he was released from the Cowboys, Septien pleaded guilty to charges of indecency with a minor; speedy wide receiver Golden Richards became addicted to painkillers after his career; wide receiver Michael Irvin, a current Cowboy, was indicted for cocaine possession last winter in a much-publicized trial.

(Before I continue, I need to take a quick pause from this litany of sleaze. There was one Cowboy whom I've admired all these years: running back Calvin Hill. He epitomized class without hiding behind a pulpit, a shiny suit, and mirrored sunglasses, or umpteen temper tantrums. And his legacy is his gentlemanly son, the Detroit Pistons' Grant Hill. Okay, that's enough of the soft stuff.)

Besides the personality and legal problems, other cracks in the Cowboys' mirage revealed themselves in

Peter Gent's classic novel *North Dallas Forty* (later made into a fine film starring Nick Nolte and Mac Davis). Gent, a former receiver, wrote a thinly disguised roman à clef of Cowboys culture and exposed the myriad pressures NFL players face, many of which involved booze and painkillers. And the feuding side of the Cowboys revealed itself with, first, the bitter Jerry Jones takeover and the exile of Landry, hat and all, and then with the bitter Jerry Jones–Jimmy Johnson feud and subsequent exile of Johnson, hair mousse and all.

While I admire misbehavior as much as the next wannabe rebel, I could never sympathize with the Cowboys' *bad* behavior. They had tried so hard to appear good that when their facade crumbled, all I could do was gloat. It turned out that they were as dysfunctional as every other family in America, and Tom Landry's hat couldn't contain all of Dallas's troubles.

Perhaps that explains the lure—good, bad, and indifferent—of the Cowboys. Like a good soap opera, the Cowboys' positives and negatives are etched broadly across the landscape of this country. Perhaps their problems are our problems. And perhaps we can learn something from their countless sleazy episodes, as well as from their many triumphs. Perhaps Jerry Jones and Deion Sanders and Hollywood Henderson and Leon Lett and Bob Hayes and Gil Brandt and Tex Schramm and Emmitt Smith and Duane Thomas are us. Perhaps the Cowboys are America's Team after all.

Nah.

CONRAD DOBLER

I WAS ONCE A Cowboy. No, not *those* Cowboys. I was a Cowboy from the University of Wyoming—out there where men are men, women are damned glad of it, the sheep are real nervous, and the number-one drink is Woolite on the rocks.

But I knew all about those other Cowboys down there in Dallas. Boy, did I know about them: When I was at Wyoming, I got more material from the Cowboys than from any other NFL club, which was the case with everyone they might be interested in drafting. They sent you programs, media guides, decals. They sent you this, they sent you that, they sent you everything—including interminable questionnaires and even a pen with the legend "Use this when you sign your Dallas contract" on the side. All of which marketed the Cowboys' mystique to potential draftees. Very well, thank you!

Their outreach program even included an 800 number for prospective draftees. That way, back in the days

---

CONRAD DOBLER was an offensive guard for ten years, playing with the St. Louis Cardinals, the New Orleans Saints, and the Buffalo Bills, and is the author of They Call Me Dirty.

before the draft was so extensively covered on TV that everyone and his brother knew who had been drafted scant seconds after his selection, college seniors could call Dallas to find out if they had, in fact, been selected. And you wonder how they signed so many free-agent rookies. Hell, right after the draft was completed, Dallas was back on the phone to those not drafted to add them to its roster.

For the Cowboys were a tight-knit organization, one built through the draft. They never traded for anyone. They wanted to take players right out of college and mold them into the type of people they wanted representing the Cowboys. It was almost like the Marines. It was as if they were saying to each new member of the Cowboys, "This is your team; it's not anyone else's. We drafted you, we'll take care of you. This is your ultimate goal, your ultimate responsibility, to be a Cowboy."

On *my* draft day, back in 1972, the Cowboys, as usual, had stockpiled their draft choices. And before I was selected in the fifth round by the St. Louis Cardinals—hell, I didn't realize at the time a *baseball* team wanted me— the Cowboys had selected nine players. I guess I just didn't fit the Dallas mold. But of those nine, only one, Robert Newhouse, played in a Dallas uniform longer than I did for the Cardinals—and four never even suited up in a Cowboys uniform.

I'll admit my first impression had been "Yeah, it would be nice to be a Cowboy and be on America's Team," because I felt that everyone respected them. But when I wasn't chosen by them, it meant they didn't have enough respect for me. My next reaction was "Well, fuck 'em. I'll show them," because basically that's what they were saying to me: "We're America's Team and you're probably not good enough or not the quality-type person we want on our team." It was an attitude that said, "You're a piece of trash, so go play for one of those *other* teams."

Everyone not chosen by the Cowboys hated them. If you didn't hate the Cowboys when you played in the NFL, I don't know what you were made of.

When I first came into the league, the big rivalry was between the Cowboys and the Redskins. The Cardinals didn't figure into it. Not yet, anyway. That first season, under coach Bob Holloway, we finished 4–9–1, a distant fourth in the Eastern Division. After the season the owner, Bill Bidwill, fired Holloway, changing the locks on his door so Holloway couldn't get his clothes out after the last game. (The same thing would happen later to his successor, Don Coryell, Bidwill being so cheap, he must have used the same locksmith who changed the old Holloway locks.)

We played the Cowboys twice in my rookie season, losing twice—27–6 in St. Louis and 33–24 in Dallas. While down in Dallas, I once again discovered, to my chagrin, why the Cowboys were different. Using their facilities and their locker room, we'd see how everyone had his own private locker with his own little sitting area—things like that. And we'd feel somehow cheated. I mean, if the Dallas Cowboys had it, why couldn't we? It was another one of their marketing ploys, one that made every opposing player dissatisfied, even disgruntled, to be playing on a team other than the Dallas Cowboys.

In 1973 Don Coryell came to the Cardinals. And although our record that season was the same as it had been in 1972, 4–9–1, it was to be the beginning of our glory days. And the rivalry then became the Cowboys, the Redskins, *and* the Cardinals. We were always in the fight for the Eastern Division championship.

And what was unique about the rivalry was that we couldn't beat the goddamned Redskins. We could beat the Cowboys, but we couldn't beat the goddamned Redskins. And the Redskins could beat the Cowboys and the Cowboys could beat the Redskins, but we just couldn't beat the Redskins.

The Giants and the Eagles? That was a day off, like a scrimmage.

Coryell loved to beat the Cowboys, because he loved the competition. And we all liked beating the Cowboys because they always had that air that they were better than us. Also, we knew that the game would be on national TV—the Cowboys would get ten games a year on TV, while we were lucky to get one, and if we got one, it was usually against the Cowboys.

Coryell would always call Dallas coach Tom Landry *Laundry,* as in *wash.* Not out of a lack of respect, because he did respect him, but because he had a lisp. In fact, Coryell's lisp was so amusing that we used to fight to get a seat for the Saturday-night speeches. Sometimes it sounded like a man who had had five or six martinis before he spoke. He used to give good speeches, but with his lisp he'd get all screwed up. It was first-class entertainment, almost like the opening act of *Saturday Night Live.*

But as much as Coryell respected Landry, he hated George Allen. Hated him because he said Allen was a "cheater." He told a story about Allen, back when he had been a coach at Whittier—the same college Nixon attended and where Coryell had succeeded Allen as head coach in the Fifties. At the time, Whittier was a rival of Santa Barbara. And Allen had an assistant with a year of eligibility left. So Allen sent him up to Santa Barbara for spring training, where the guy ended up being their quarterback and playing two or three games for Santa Barbara. And winning them. But, as Coryell told the story, the week Santa Barbara was supposed to play Whittier, the quarterback just disappeared. And, lo and behold, when Santa Barbara came down to play Whittier, this guy was standing on the other sideline, next to Allen, and later played against Santa Barbara.

But he never hated Landry, or *Laundry,* who had never coached in the college ranks, like Allen had, and carried no such baggage.

So our rivalry was with both the Redskins and the Cowboys—or, as they called themselves, America's Team. Boy, did they have those guys in the media bamboozled. They bought that America's Team crap and would write about how the Cowboys were a great team and what great individuals they were. I spent two days with a couple of them at a football camp one summer, big-name players who thought they were tough. These guys ran hard—very, very hard—on about an hour's sleep. They were wild men, just like us. They wanted the same things we did: to drink a little booze, to smoke a little dope, to get a little tail. So where did they get this America's Team crap from?

Whenever, heaven forbid, they were caught doing anything, the Cowboy organization would cover it up. Look at what got into the newspapers about some of the Cowboys—Cowboys like Hollywood Henderson, Lance Rentzel, and Bob Hayes. Can you imagine how bad it was if *that* was reported? The Cowboys did such a good job of covering their tracks in the Dallas–Fort Worth area that if that got out, think of all the things that didn't.

Maybe that's why the media bought that America's Team stuff. They didn't know about all the Cowboy shenanigans. Or else they needed "America's Team" more than the country did—someone to build up so that later they could take them down.

But they were the same as the rest of us, believe me, even if they did view themselves as the privileged class. However, we players on other teams looked at them and said, "Hey, they're the same kind of jerk-offs we are, but they never get written up. We do when we get our noses dirty. Why?" You know why? Because the media bought their image, their marketing, their mystique.

It always seemed that the Cowboys were being held out to the public as outstanding citizens and righteous Christians. They never cursed, never did this, never did that. But they were just as wild a bunch as everybody else. Only their image, courtesy of the press, was different.

Maybe the media felt so strongly about having something and someone to look up to that they didn't want to tarnish the Cowboys' image in any way whatsoever. Of course, success had a lot to do with their—along with most of the people in America for whom the Cowboys were America's Team—perception of what was right and wrong. Remember, perception is reality.

And whenever we played against them, we always felt like the bad guys, the ones dressed in black, like we were Darth Vader or something. We'd always be sitting there saying, "Shit, man, I don't remember designating them America's Team."

I disliked everything about the Cowboys: the team, their players, their "no-roof" roof, and their self-righteous assumed name, "America's Team." I mean, if they were dressed in gray Confederate uniforms, how could they be America's Team? We had that war once, and they lost.

Well, maybe there was one thing I didn't dislike: the Dallas Cowboy Cheerleaders. They were good, they were beautiful, and they loved to show off their titties. If you were a man's man and possessed the normal dosage of testosterone, you couldn't play a helluva lot of football with all that stuff running around the field.

How much of a distraction were they? Once, when Jim Hanifan, then the offensive-line coach of the Cardinals, was conducting pregame warm-ups, the Dallas cheerleaders came running by, doing *their* warm-ups. As head after head rose to get a good "look-see," Hanifan, in resignation, shook his head and said, "Fuck, man, let's just watch them go by and then let's get back to warming up."

Then there was the time during a game down in Dallas, with the defensive unit out on the field when Dan Dierdorf, Tom Banks, and I were sitting on the bench along with the rest of the offensive team. Back in those days, we were somewhat of an offensive powerhouse; defensively, we sucked. Usually when the opposing team is third-and-15, you'd get up and start stretching, preparing to go back into the game. However, we knew full well that our defense couldn't hold water and that we weren't going back in until the other team scored. So why watch them?

And here come the Dallas cheerleaders, dancing and prancing past our bench. And as they do, all three of us are watching the cheerleaders, not the field. Well, wouldn't you know it, the television cameras zeroed in on us and the name DOBLER on the back of my jersey was there in full view for everyone out there in TV land to see. One of those who did was my ex-wife, and I never heard the end of it. Yes, they had nice cheerleaders, I'll give them that!

But besides the Dallas Cowboy Cheerleaders, I disliked everything else about them. Most of all, I disliked Lee Roy Jordan.

When I first came into the league, Dallas was employing something called the Flex defense. Simply stated, the Flex was a variation of the basic "4-3" defense with one strong-side defensive end or one weak-side tackle dropping back two yards off the line of scrimmage into a reading, or Flex, position. All of which made blocking assignments much more difficult as we tried to pick up these defenders, which inevitably left holes in our front line for their linebackers to shoot through.

Many times when Dallas used the Flex against us, defensive tackle Jethro Pugh would line up on my nose. Now, Jethro Pugh was like a day off for me. Pugh would eat up other guards who might have been better than I was, but I had Jethro's number and knew that I was going to win 90 percent of our battles.

Well, Pugh or no Pugh, their Flex worked so well against us that more often than not their middle linebacker, Jordan, would fill in and come through the hole, getting into our backfield.

However, we caught on to that manuever and knew how to defense their defense, so to speak. There was this one time when Pugh was up on my nose and I blocked him and went through and picked up Jordan, catching him under the chin and putting him on his back with a pretty good shot. I kind of got my fist under his chinstrap, and as I'm lying on top of him, my fist is grinding into his chin. Well, Jordan grabbed my wrist and bit my thumb. He probably would have bitten it clean through, but his top retainer came out. And there I was, thinking, "Shit, man, this is the Dallas Cowboys. This is America's Team. And this guy bites me. I guess this is the way the game is supposed to be played."

And from that magic moment in my rookie year, I not

only got the reputation for being the dirtiest player in the NFL but also got baptized into the league with the same tactics people accused me of using. Imagine the holy Christian attitude these motherfuckers had! Sort of ironic.

I was stuck with that label, the "NFL's Dirtiest Player," after the Jordan incident. One time later in my career, I was called up to the NFL offices in New York to answer some charge or other. Well, the night before I'm supposed to show up, I'm at this bar in New York called, I think, the Tittle Tattle or somesuch, where the Giants used to go. And wouldn't you know it? While I'm sitting there minding my own business, two Giants, John Hicks and Jack Gregory, get into this big fight. And I'm just sitting there, drinking and watching them go at it. Someone called over to me and said, "Why don't you break it up, Dobler?" Well, if it had been a fight between a Cardinal and a Giant, I would have jumped in. But these were two Giants, so let *them* solve it.

Anyway, I had to meet with Commissioner Rozelle at eight the next morning. So I get back to the hotel at five, just in time to shower and show up. I've got this big defense planned to counter their charges of playing rough and to support my side of protecting the quarterback—all sorts of newspaper articles about quarterbacks who had been knocked out of games and what their teams had done after their injuries. So I show up at the NFL offices on Park Avenue at the appointed hour and a secretary gives me a cup of coffee and a morning newspaper. And there, in headlines on the front page, is DOBLER INVOLVED IN FIGHT WITH TWO GIANTS AT THE TITTLE TATTLE. What is Rozelle going to think? Here I'm supposed to meet him at eight in the morning and, at least according to the paper, I'm in a fight with two guys in a bar four hours before our meeting.

Soon I'm called into the viewing room, where they rack up a reel of film showing me doing the many evil things I'm supposed to have done in the past six or seven games—a late hit here, a punch there, a trip here and there, and a leg whip everywhere, etc., etc., etc. And as I watched the film, I slid lower and lower in my seat with each incident shown. Soon I could hardly see the seat in front of me. At this point Rozelle turned to me and said, "What do you have to say about all of this?" And all I could think to retort was "You could have made that film up on anybody in the NFL." Now both Rozelle and Art McNally, the supervisor of officials, who was there, too, looked at me and said, "But we didn't. We made it up on you."

So they fined me $1,800. Everyone else they had called for similar offensive "offenses" was fined, too; but my fine was the heaviest. I figured, let me pay up and get the hell out of here. After all, they had spent more than $1,800 to make up this film and I'm not going to buck them—they had far more resources than I had.

Want another example of those wonderful Christian gentlemen they call America's Team? Against the Cowboys we ran a play on which we pulled everyone on the off side and caught their linebacker, Lee Roy Jordan, trying to come through the back hole in an attempt to disrupt the pitch from behind. In the NFL you have a three-yard area on each side of the line of scrimmage called dead man's territory. Anything goes in this area, including hand-to-hand combat. In other words, it's trench warfare at close quarters. And so, as the play developed, Jordan, who had been trying to get through the hole, had fallen to his knees by accident and people were stampeding his way. Now, if you're in a position to get clipped, you're going to get a knee injury. Well, Jordan got both—clipped and a knee injury. As he was being dragged off the field, he could be heard shouting, "You motherfucking, cocksucking, mother-cheating bastard!" And we all stood there thinking, "Well, that's America's Team for you." Wonder what Tom Landry thought of such language?

As my career wound down, I wound up in Buffalo, where one of my teammates was Phil Villapiano, who had once been a member of the Oakland Raiders. Phil told me that Oakland coach John Madden had put out a fifty-dollar bounty on me—fifty dollars for anyone who could knock me out of a game. Now, fifty dollars may not sound like a lot to you, but it was for the Raiders. Those bastards would have killed their mother for fifty dollars.

It was while I was playing for the Bills that I got a refresher course in what America's Team was really all about. The year was 1981, the year the Cowboys lost to the 49ers in the NFC championship game on a last-second pass from Joe Montana to Dwight Clark. After the game, Landry and several members of the Dallas press corps, almost all of whom were mere puppets of the Cowboys' publicity office, began whining about how the Cowboys never would have lost had it not been for an injury to their defensive tackle John Dutton—who, not incidentally, had been one of the very few players Dallas had ever traded for. The injury, they claimed, had been inflicted by one Conrad Dobler in the tenth game of the season. And, they went on, Dobler should be kicked out of the league because if he hadn't injured Dutton, we—not San Francisco—would be in the Super Bowl. What bullshit, I thought to myself. How low can the Dallas Cowboys go? From being America's Team to blaming their inability to advance to the Super Bowl on an injury in Week 10, not on Dwight Clark's catch?

That, to me, is the essence of the Dallas Cowboys: a

bullshit organization that hides behind its arrogant, self-righteous name of America's Team and possesses none of the qualities that America aspires to.

In the old days they just looked down on you as if you were some second-class citizen. Today they combine old-fashioned arrogance with new-fangled earrings, tattoos, *Superfly* clothing, and drug use, guns, rape, and more. But bottom line: America's Team, the former kings of the NFL, have no clothes. Never had, never will. They are anything but America's Team.

LARRY FELSER

IT'S NOT A MATTER of mere loathing that sets so many molars to grinding over the Dallas Cowboys, it's the smugness, overbearance, imperiousness, and downright pretense with which they go about achieving their successes.

Beano Cook, the sporting laureate of Pittsburgh, might have struck the right chord some years ago when he paid a compliment—left-handed though it may have been—to Tex Schramm, the man who virtually invented the Cowboys.

"Tex," said Beano, "in my estimation, the Dallas Cowboys are the second most efficient organization of the twentieth century."

"Why, thank you, Beano," said Schramm, blushing modestly. "By the way, who's in first ahead of us?"

"The Third Reich."

In Buffalo, "City Without Pretensions," there is a special attitude toward Dallas that sets municipal teeth to grinding. It is the ultimate in Rust Belt–Sun Belt comparisons.

Dallas has Mexico, just a long afternoon's drive down

LARRY FELSER is the sports editor of the Buffalo News *and past president of the Pro Football Writers Association.*

Interstate 35, which puts the jalapeño in its chili. Canada is just across the Peace Bridge from Buffalo, and thousands of visitors come daily to sample the chicken wings and beef on weck, a delicious, salted roll brought to western New York by German immigrants more than a century ago. Dallas, from an architectural viewpoint, is one vast shopping mall. Buffalo is full of Olmsted parks, great buildings designed by Louis Sullivan and E. B. Green, and Frank Lloyd Wright houses.

Buffalo boasts two Presidents, Grover Cleveland and (well, okay) Millard Fillmore. Dallas has Ross Perot. Buffalo was the site of the assassination of President William McKinley at the Pan-American Exposition in 1901. Dallas has its infamous Dealey Plaza. Dallas celebrates the urban cowboy with getups that include Western belt buckles as massive as Lancelot's shield. There are Buffalonians who celebrate Dingus Day clad in bowling shirts.

Okay, we're a tad down at the heels. They're Neiman-Marcus. The football crowds watching the Cowboys at Texas Stadium are more like theater audiences. Some of our crazies strip to the waist while watching the Bills play December games in Rich Stadium.

That's where this argument has been fought out, on football fields. Everyone knows that the Bills lost four consecutive Super Bowls, which became a punch line on late-night television. Dallas pounded Buffalo, 52–17, in Super Bowl XXVII and won again the next year, 30–13, in Super Bowl XXVIII. Yet the Cowboys, for all their glory, never made it to four consecutive Super Bowls. Besides, the Bills refused to stay down after they were knocked down. They kept getting up to fight again, which is a civic trait in Buffalo.

That's what is so maddening about the Cowboys' haughtiness. They haven't suffered enough to qualify for all their success. There should be an established period of pain before a team is eligible for long runs of success.

The Cowboys actually had a winless season, their pioneer year, 1960. In fact, it took seven years before they had a winning record, but they were an NFL expansion team then, and all expansion teams have growing pains. They are expected to be terrible; at least they were until free agency made instant monsters of Carolina and Jacksonville.

The only other time the Cowboys finished dead last in the NFL, 1988, they had Cowboys' luck: The consolation prize was the first pick in the next draft, Troy Aikman, the best quarterback available in six years. If the dead season had occurred a year before, the 'Boys would have had their pick of Vinny Testaverde or Kelly Stouffer. One year later no team even bothered to pick a quarterback until the third round.

Except for that massive stroke of good fortune, Jimmy Johnson's pompadour would have gone flaccid.

The truth is, the Bills have had as many last-place seasons as the Cowboys have had Super Bowl victories, five. The first time Buffalo sank into the subbasement, 1968, O. J. Simpson was the consolation prize. Three seasons later, even with Simpson, the Bills finished last again, and over the course of the 1970 and 1971 seasons, they went seventeen games between victories.

Yet during one of those house-of-horror seasons, Buffalo experienced the pure joy of watching the Cowboys in an exquisite humiliation.

It was 1984, the year the Buffalo defense allowed a record 454 points, sixty points more than they allowed at their previous nadir. When the opposition churns out an average of four touchdowns a game, you'd better have some explosion coming out of your cannon. What came out of the Bills' cannon was a little red flag with

BANG! printed on it. In six of their sixteen games, they scored ten or fewer points. They also committed every weird infraction known to football since the days of Amos Alonzo Stagg. They found ways to lose that would have baffled Pop Warner. They employed players who would have advanced Gloomy Gil Doby into manic depression.

The Bills' faithful, who had witnessed their heroes losing four of the last five games the previous season to flutter out of playoff contention, did not find this amusing. In the previous three home games, Rich Stadium was not even close to being half filled. In the home game after Dallas came to town, the Bills and Colts drew 20,693—64,000 fewer than observed the Cowboys on that fateful day, November 18.

Dallas hadn't played in Buffalo in thirteen years, back when the Bills performed in War Memorial Stadium, a mausoleum constructed by the WPA during Franklin Roosevelt's second term. When the Cowboys play in foreign and unfamiliar territory, it is a festival of front-runners, people who pull for Anheuser-Busch over the local microbrewery; Wal-Mart over Vic and Sade's hardware; Italy over Ethiopia.

That day they came from all directions: Cow Chip, Pennsylvania; Bumpkin's Corners, Indiana; Moose Bladder, Ontario. None of them knew where the hell they were going, which caused the mother of all traffic jams.

Normally, I arrive at the stadium about an hour ahead of time to do some schmoozing and get my game face on. Not this day. I was at least two miles from my usual parking space when I encountered gridlock, created by people in vans and station wagons with "Cowboys über Alles" signs protruding from their windows.

I maneuvered down side streets, through back alleys, over front lawns until finally I reached a point where I was past the stadium but at least could see it. All of a sudden . . . an opening! I did a quick U-ie and shifted down to daylight. I was pointed in the right direction! The problem was that I stayed in that same spot for forty-five minutes with androids surrounding me, shouting, "Buffalo sucks."

When the mass of traffic began moving once again, it was at a glacial pace. As kickoff time grew nearer, so did my loathing for America's Team. Whose America? The America of the robber barons, Quantrill and his Raiders, Lizzie Borden? The America of Simon Legree, Boss Tweed, and Ma Barker? Of Pruneface, Barnacle Bill, and the Penguin?

I was working myself into a premium game face before I turned in to the parking lot. I thought of Danny White shredding the Bills' flimsy secondary; of Bills tacklers playing flag football as Tony Dorsett zoomed by; of Randy White brutalizing an aging Joe Ferguson. As I locked my car door, I could hear the National Anthem.

I missed the opening kickoff. I *never* miss opening kickoffs. Buffalo received, and as usual, things began on a negative note, since the Bills were on their own 15-yard line as I reached the top of the stairs on the way down to my seat. Halfway down the stairs, something shocking happened. Shocking and satisfying and ecstatically beautiful.

A large hole opened in the Dallas defensive line. A backup guard, a lunch-bucket free agent named Tim Vogler, blocked Randy White out of the way. Through the hole came Greg Bell of the Bills, and he was—could this be a delusion as a result of inhaling all those exhaust fumes?—in the clear!

Bell was a rookie that year, Buffalo's first-round selection in the draft after an injury-pocked career at Notre Dame. He was one of the few sunny days on that horrible team, gaining more than 1,000 yards. He would be a disappointment after that, a talented player but a "sometimes" guy. He would shine briefly, then recede into the shadows. But on this day, he would do something unforgettable. Once in the clear, he accelerated. When it became obvious that no Cowboy was going to catch him, there was a mighty cheer from the minority (in this case, the home fans) as mouths shut and chins dropped in those sections crammed with the Lone Star contingent. All the way, 85 yards; no flags. Buffalo 7, Dallas 0.

It was your classic rock-'em-on-their-heels moment. The Cowboys never recovered. They had some chances, but it seemed a conspiracy of the fates that roles would be reversed this day. Everything the 'Boys tried turned to horsepucky. They never did score a touchdown the entire afternoon. The final score was 14–3. The front-runner tourists silently filed out of Rich Stadium and back to Bumpkin's Corners, Cow Chip, and Moose Bladder.

There have been happier embalming chambers than the Dallas locker room. Dorsett sat in front of his locker with his head in his hands. "This is the darkest day in the history of the Dallas Cowboys," he murmured. How sweet it was!

The loss poured axle grease into the punch bowl for the Cowboys' silver anniversary season. It also cost them the playoffs, the first time in ten years they hadn't played in the postseason.

The next Sunday the Bills went down to Washington and got drilled by the Redskins, 41–14. *Machs nicht.* They and their followers would be warmed all season and beyond by the memory of the day America's Stuffedshirts had been mortified.

Nothing could top that one for Cowboy-haters. But there was a nice reprise in the second game of the 1993 season, eight months after Buffalo had been barbecued by Dallas, 52–17, in Super Bowl XXVII. The 'Boys couldn't even pull that one off cleanly. Leon Lett, the massive defensive tackle, picked up a loose ball and ran three-quarters the length of the field for what would have been another touchdown. But Leon couldn't resist hotdogging it inside the 5-yard line.

Don Beebe of the Bills, a graduate of the never-give-up school, pursued Lett all the way, and when Lett raised his arms, with the ball held in one hand, Beebe hacked it away and Dallas lost possession.

The rematch was in Texas Stadium the following September 12. The Dallas crowd settled into their seats, smugly, to watch Blowout II. Instead, it was a defensive rumble, with Buffalo holding a 13–10 lead going into the final minute.

Dallas had possession and Troy Aikman was leading a relentless march, as he had earlier in the game when the Cowboys marched 98 yards to get back into contention. This time the winning touchdown seemed inevitable. So inevitable that Cowboys owner Jerry Jones had slipped into the shadows of the end zone tunnel, ready to sashay between the goalposts and raise his arms in a reptilian declaration of victory, which was his custom.

Aikman launched the pass toward his most reliable target, tight end Jay Novacek, who had worked his way into touchdown position. Then at the last second, a rookie dime back for Buffalo, Matt Darby, leaped in front of Novacek, clutched the ball, and fell to the ground with the game-saving interception.

As this happened, Jones was caught mid-preen, his arms half raised. Quickly, he turned and slinked back into the shadows. The Forces of Evil had been frustrated once again.

BILL GALLO

THE IDEA HERE IS to say why and how much I hate the Dallas Cowboys. I'll have to admit, right off, that I do not, in fact, hate them—but I will have to come clean to one little annoyance: Why should they call themselves America's Team?

Why aren't the Giants America's Team? Is not Rutherford, New Jersey, part of America? Hey, even if you don't like New Jersey, how about Pittsburgh, where good ol' American steel is produced?

You can make Denver America's Team. Or any other NFL franchise in the country, for that matter. Every damned team in the league is America's Team, and that's what we should call *all* of them.

Better yet, let's abandon the term altogether. Let's keep "America's Team" a bunch of the favorite cowboys we've known through the years—not that Dallas football team, but those familiar cowpokes you see sketched on the next page.

———————

BILL GALLO is America's premier sports cartoonist. His work has appeared in the New York Daily News *for the past thirty-seven years and he is the winner of ten National Cartoon Society awards and twenty-one Front Page awards.*

MIKE GOLIC

LET ME ADMIT, RIGHT at the outset, that I was never, ever a Dallas Cowboys fan. Going all the way back to my childhood in Cleveland, I just couldn't stand them. I really don't know what it was that made me dislike them so. Maybe it was that they were supposed to be this "great" team. Or maybe it was that I just couldn't take Roger Staubach, the old national hero, or Bob Lilly or Tony Dorsett—and there was just something about Harvey Martin I couldn't stomach. Or maybe it was that everybody was always calling them America's Team. And I thought to myself, "What crap! Who died and elected them king anyway?"

Whatever it was, it was to be, as they said at the end of the movie *Casablanca,* the beginning of a beautiful relationship: a lifelong hate-hate relationship with the Cowboys. One that would sustain me throughout my pro career.

My first port of call in the pros was the Houston Oilers—the Cowboys' cross-state rival, I guess you could

---

MIKE GOLIC was a defensive lineman for the Houston Oilers, the Philadelphia Eagles, and the Miami Dolphins from 1984 through 1993.

say. But whatever I felt for the Cowboys as a member of the Oilers was nothing to what I would feel with my second pro team, the Philadelphia Eagles.

There I played for Buddy Ryan, and to hear Buddy rant about the Cowboys was like a fireman pouring gasoline on a burning house. He hated the Cowboys and knew how to pump up his team against the 'Boys, fueling the Eagles' hatred for them. He didn't want us to just beat the Cowboys, he wanted us to beat *up* the Cowboys. He wanted us to fight, to kick, to scratch, to punch, to do whatever we had to do to beat them. And the good thing about it was that we had the people to do it: We had Clyde Simmons and Reggie White, two of the best bookends around; we had Seth Joyner at linebacker; Eric Allen and Byron Evans in the middle; Mike Pitts and myself at tackles; and Jerome Brown, God rest his soul, at defensive tackle. We were just stacked on the defensive side of the ball.

I joined the Eagles mid-season in 1987—that was the strike season, if you'll remember. For the duration of the strike, the NFL teams all used replacement players—or "scabs," as Buddy called them. He was openly disdainful of them, barely bothering to coach them. And while his attitude may have helped build team loyalty among the regulars, who were sitting out the strike, it did nothing for the replacement players, who lost all their games— including one to the Cowboys, who ran up the score on the replacement Eagles, beating them good, 41–22.

Now, Buddy is one of those guys who never forgets, always tucking a memory or two in his back pocket for future use. That future use came two games later, after the strike had been settled. And it was vintage Buddy Ryan.

Buddy not only wanted to trash Dallas, he wanted his

pound of flesh to avenge their having humiliated *his* Eagles—replacements or not—in their first matchup. And was he to get it! With the game all but over, we had both a ten-point lead and the ball. Normally the team with the lead in the final seconds of the game has its quarterback kneel down with the ball to run out the clock. But not this time. Our quarterback, Randall Cunningham, was doing the ol' "kneel-down" for the first three downs. On the last of his supposed "kneel-downs," Randall took the snap and faked like he was going down. Then he straightened up and threw a bomb for a touchdown, giving us a 37–20 victory. And Buddy just trotted off the field, laughing all the way.

You want to talk about setting hate in stone? That one game cemented the Eagles-Cowboys rivalry for all time.

The Eagles continued their dominance over the Cowboys in 1988, beating them twice in a streak that would ultimately run to eight straight Philadelphia wins over Dallas. But if one game defined Buddy's philosophy of not only beating them but beating them up, it was the second game of the 1989 season.

By 1989 the Cowboys had had a changing of the guard. Their new head coach was now Jimmy Johnson, who had replaced Tom Landry to become only the second head coach in Cowboy history. None of the Eagles particularly cared for Johnson and his carefully sculpted hair. And one Eagle in particular, yours truly, Mike Golic, disliked him more than most—a hatred built on the Notre Dame–Miami rivalry, his having been the coach at the University of Miami when I was playing for Notre Dame. And so it was with a double dose of pleasure that I relished our two wins over Dallas in 1989, 27–0 and 20–10.

But it was that first game, the 27–0 one played on

Thanksgiving Day in Dallas, that more than anything fanned the flames of the Eagles-Cowboys rivalry.

But first some background: The Eagles had had a placekicker at the beginning of the year named Luis Zendejas. Earlier in the season, we had played back-to-back away games against Denver and San Diego. And instead of returning to Philly from Denver and then going back out to the coast to play San Diego, we just went out to San Diego and stayed there the week before our game against the Chargers. After the Denver game but before the San Diego game, Buddy, unhappy with Zendejas's kicking—he had made just 14 of his 24 field-goal attempts—cut him from the squad. Just cut him in Denver. Well, Zendejas was not happy with this turn of events and proceeded to rip Buddy up one side and down the other, calling him every name in the book. And as I said before, Buddy never forgets.

By the time of our Thanksgiving Day game against the Cowboys, Zendejas had been signed by Dallas and given the kickoff assignment. Despite Buddy's pleas of innocence, many are still convinced that he had assigned a "bounty hunter" to get even with Zendejas—and that the instrument for his revenge was Jessie Small, a rookie linebacker. His job: get Zendejas on the opening kickoff.

As Zendejas teed up the ball for the kickoff, Small stood on the front line, just ten yards away from the kickoff tee, watching Zendejas's every move. On the kickoff, the rest of the Eagles fell back to set up the return. But Small seemingly couldn't have cared less where the ball went, he just made a beeline for Zendejas and absolutely crushed him, spinning him around and depositing him, in little pieces, around the midfield marker. After a few seconds, Zendejas struggled to his feet and started to walk on legs that were strangers to each other in the direction of the Eagles' bench, his helmet almost sideways on his head, peering out the earhole and cursing a blue streak in the direction of Buddy. And Buddy was just standing there, laughing at this picture of the late-Saturday-night drunkard, a helmet resting crookedly on his head, yelling at him. Finally, several Cowboys raced across the field to gather in Zendejas and direct him back to their bench—all the while shouting some obscenities of their own at Buddy.

After the game—which became known as the Bounty Bowl—charges and countercharges flew. An infuriated Jimmy Johnson accused the Eagles of putting a price on Zendejas's head. And Zendejas insisted he had proof of such a bounty in the form of a taped telephone conversation with Eagles special-teams coach Al Roberts, who supposedly had warned Zendejas of the upcoming attack. But Buddy merely wondered aloud why anyone would want to knock a kicker out of the game who had been in a six-week slump.

But even though the Zendejas incident on the opening kickoff created the headlines, the rest of the game belonged to the Eagles' defensive line. At the time, we had a defensive line made up of Reggie White, Clyde Simmons, Jerome Brown, Mike Pitts, and me. Jerome was about 315, Reggie was probably 310, both Mike and I were 290–295, and Clyde was probably the lightest, at 285–290. So we had some size on our side of the line. Enough that defensive line coach Dale Haupt would say to us, "If you can't line up over somebody and beat his ass, then you don't belong in the league."

The asses we had to beat that afternoon were the big ones belonging to the Dallas offensive line. Mark Tuinei was probably the smallest, at about 275–280; the rest of them weighed in at 315 and up. All they did was come flying off the ball, trying to drive you into the cheap seats.

And on that afternoon we "beat their asses," hammering them all day long with a straight-ahead four-man rush. All told, we had eleven and a half sacks. And although I was known as a run stopper, I had two and a half of them. It was one of the sweetest victories of my career.

But the game that day wasn't just a game, it was— starting with Small's opening-kickoff decimation of Zendejas—an all-out war. I mean, here it was Thanksgiving Day and most people were just sitting in front of their TV sets, burping up their turkey dinner, and what did they get to help them digest their meal but one of the dirtiest football games ever played!

There were full-fledged fights going on everywhere you looked. It was sheer madness. Everybody was all over the field throwing punches, and the referees were throwing flags. One fight started on about the 10-yard line and worked its way clear to the back of the end zone. And there, almost in the stands, could be seen big Jerome Brown and even bigger Kevin Gogan of the Cowboys (tale of the tape: Brown, six-two, 315, versus Gogan, six-seven, 320) squaring off like two boxers and dancing around like Holyfield and Tyson, punching each other—with face masks on, no less. And the Dallas loonies in the stands were raining beer down on Jerome, drenching him. Obviously, none were stupid enough to come down out of the stands and challenge Jerome, or they would have had their asses put where their heads were. Not that they would have known the difference.

The referees finally restored order, of sorts, tossing out a couple of combatants, Mike Pitts included, and clearing the field. During the donnybrook one of those ubiquitous cameras milling around on the perimeter of the melee caught me using a couple of choice four-letter words. After the game my ma called and asked, "What are you doing swearing on national TV?" "Ma," I tried to explain, "we were playing the Cowboys. You can't help but cuss at them guys because you hate them!"

That's what it was every time the Eagles played the Cowboys: pure and unadulterated hate. Hate to the point of actually trying to hurt each other. You tried to step on somebody's hand, knee somebody in the back; they tried to go for someone's knees. These two teams had it in for each other.

That hate carried over to the coaches, Buddy Ryan and Jimmy Johnson. They couldn't stand each other. Most coaches, as I'm sure you've noticed, at least try to be friendly to their fellow fraternity members, even if it's all an act. Not Ryan and Johnson. Buddy would say to us, "These guys can't beat us. They don't have the talent we do. We're going to walk all over them." Our place, their place, it didn't matter. And Ryan didn't give a rat's ass if Johnson talked the same way about him and the Eagles.

And the fans? The Philly fans are the most rabid in the world. They love you when you're playing well and hate you when you're playing poorly. And they hated the Dallas Cowboys more than any team in the NFL. Woe be to any misguided Dallas fan wearing a Cowboy jersey and wandering around Veterans Stadium on the day of a Philadelphia-Dallas game. He was always in danger of grave bodily harm. Or, at the very least, having his T-shirt made into an instant dishrag.

All season long, like a hunting dog spotting a pheasant, Eagle fans would point toward the Cowboy home game at the Vet. It was the highlight of the Eagles' schedule.

And leading up to the game, the media would get into the act, feeding them story after story—"The Big Game" or "How to Prepare for the Cowboys" or "Beat the 'Boys"—further inciting them. As if they needed anything more to hate the Cowboys.

Take the 1992 season. The Eagles had begun with three straight wins, and everyone—at least everyone in Philadelphia—was predicting that there was a Super Bowl in our future. They had good reason: After all, our defense had led the NFC in 1991 in fewest total yards, fewest rushing yards, and fewest passing yards, only the fifth time a team had ever achieved that hat trick. And we had squashed John Elway and the Denver Broncos for our third win, 30–0.

As fate and the schedule makers would have it, our next opponent was Dallas. At home. On *Monday Night Football.*

The Cowboys were also 3–0, so the game became more than just the ordinary run-of-the-mill Eagles-Cowboys war—it became, at least in the mind of almost everyone in Philadelphia, a preview of the NFC title game. And with a bye week between the Denver and Dallas games, the buildup for this so-called showdown was unreal.

One all-sports radio station in Philly, WIP, not only devoted two weeks to this buildup, but on the day of the game began its pregame show at eight in the morning. And remember, this was a Monday-*night* game.

As we did every night before a home game, the Eagles stayed in a hotel in town, all the better to be able to concentrate on the game and assemble for our last-minute team meeting and trip to the stadium. But since the Dallas game wasn't until nine that night, Buddy allowed us to go home for a while after the team meeting. So there I was, on the highway driving home and listening to WIP, when all of a sudden, right in front of me, an eighteen-wheeler clipped the rear end of a car and sent it spinning off onto the highway divider. The car, now out of control, flipped over on the grass two or three times, but fortunately, landed right side up. I pulled over to the side of the road and sprinted to the disabled vehicle to see if I could be of assistance. And as I neared the car, I could hear the car radio, blaring loud and clear. There was no mistaking the sound: It was the WIP pregame show.

As I got closer to the disabled car, I could see that the driver was a mess. There was blood coming out of his head and he was slumped over the wheel. And I thought to myself, "My God, this guy's dead. . . ." But luckily, he had his seat belt on. And as I reached in, I could see he was moving—well, sort of—and I shouted, "Hey, hey . . . buddy, you alright?" At that, he looked up and saw me and muttered, "Hey, you're Mike Golic . . . I've got tickets for the game tonight . . . I can't wait for the game. . . ." And, with that, he took off his seat belt and tried to get out of the car. All I thought to say was, "Wow . . . buddy, just relax, your car just flipped over three times . . . chill out. . . ." Finally, after what seemed like hours but was in reality only a few minutes, the police arrived and I tried to explain to them what happened. Meanwhile, this guy was just chattering away, "I'll be at the game tonight . . . I'm going to the game tonight . . ." over and over again. And I stood there thinking, "Man, this guy doesn't know where the hell he is . . . he's clueless."

Well, to make a long story longer, we beat Dallas 31–7, and the next week I was sitting with my family at a local restaurant. At the end of the meal, the waitress who had been serving us said, "This meal's on me." I thanked her and asked why. She responded, "That was my uncle in the accident you helped." I asked, "How is he? Is he still in the hospital?" "Oh, no," she answered, "they took him to the hospital, but he said, 'No way. I'm going to the game,' and just walked out and went."

That, to me, epitomizes the loyalty of Philly fans—or, as they're known in Philadelphia, Philly Phanatics. Nothing, but nothing, will stand between them and their love for the Eagles. Especially when their beloved Eagles are playing the hated Cowboys.

Although we had gotten off to a promising start in 1992, by mid-season we had run into some potholes, losing four games in six weeks—including a hard-fought loss to the Cowboys down in Dallas. However, by the end of the season, with our offense led by a comebacking Randall Cunningham and newly acquired Herschel Walker and our defense once again leading the league in most categories, we got back on the road to the playoffs, finishing out the season just as we had started it, with four straight wins. Now, after clobbering New Orleans in the first round of the playoffs, we prepared to face Dallas again in a rubber match for the right to play in the NFC championship.

Our practice sessions during the week leading up to the Dallas game were hardly the stuff of ordinary practices, those half-speed run-throughs that preceded normal, run-of-the-mill games. Hell no, this was Dallas Cowboys Week, and we ran the plays full-tilt, almost as in "You'd better strap it up 'cause we're going to hit you, going to belt you." They were more intense and more difficult than any other practices during the year. We wanted to hit people that week, hit them as if they were Dallas Cowboys. And a lot of fights broke out as offensive linemen finally tired of being swatted around by defensive linemen as if *they* were Dallas Cowboys.

Somehow it worked. By the end of the week, we had come together as a team. And then we had a common goal: to go play that team with the star on their helmets and rip it off and stuff it up their asses and let them know that they weren't America's Team.

By the time we arrived in Dallas we were confident—maybe overconfident—of victory. There was no way we were going to lose. No way! In fact, our confidence was such that we came running out onto the field before the pregame warm-ups and went to every corner of Texas Stadium to jeer their fans, trying to rile up those good ol' Bubbas, many of whom were so mad that they almost wet their pants in an effort to get at us. We were so sky high, we were screaming up into the stands, making "noise" and using some of our best "worst" language as we jawed with them, telling them, "Stick it up your grits." Or something like that.

However, it all turned out to be just noise, as the Cowboys clobbered us, 34–10, and went on to win both the NFC championship and the Super Bowl.

No matter that we lost to Dallas, I still couldn't accept them as America's Team. Not then, not now, not ever.

I mean, where do they come off calling themselves America's Team anyway? It's almost as if the Cowboys, the media, the whole stupid city of Dallas, and the whole stinking state of Texas were saying to all of us, "You're playing America's Team this week, my friend. You're playing the best there is." And I thought, "Wait a minute. Who in hell said they were the best? They aren't the best. And they sure as shit aren't America's Team." And I hated them, the city, and the state for thinking they were better than anybody else.

I guess that's my biggest problem. As a professional athlete, I don't think anybody is better than me. That arrogant Dallas Cowboy way of thinking they're America's Team, America's sweethearts, drives me nuts. I just want them to shut up. And I want to do something about it. I want to beat them, to humiliate them, to rip that goddamned star off their helmets.

And every time we'd beat the Cowboys, I'd say, "There's a blow for everybody who isn't a Cowboy, who isn't up there on the pedestal, who isn't called 'the best.'"

They're no more America's Team than the Eagles are. And there was nothing sweeter than beating the team that some stupid people call America's Team—as the Eagles did nine of the twelve times we played them when I was there. Nothing!

DEACON JONES

THE DALLAS COWBOYS WERE part of Deacon Jones's personal life almost right from the very start, in Los Angeles, down to the end in Washington—and even beyond, into Canton.

I first came in contact, literally, with the Dallas Cowboys back in 1963. That was the year when the Cowboys, then an expansion team in only their fourth year of existence, moved their training camp to Thousand Oaks, California, only a short hop, skip, and bus ride from the Rams' training facility at Chapman College in the city of Orange. And every day the two teams would scrimmage together in the 100-degree heat, one day at their training camp, the next day at ours.

Back then they were led by their quarterback, little Eddie LeBaron, probably the smallest man ever to play pro football. Some say he was five foot eight. No way he was five-eight. He had to be five-one, maybe closer to

DAVID "DEACON" JONES was a defensive end for the Los Angeles Rams, the San Diego Chargers, and the Washington Redskins from 1961 through 1974. He is a member of the Football Hall of Fame and was selected as a member of the NFL "All-Time" team.

four-nine. But the little guy had guts, an excellent passing arm, and a great knowledge of the game. And despite his size, he could see the whole field and was a great leader under duress.

Over the next few years I watched as the Cowboys grew—both in terms of talent and in development—until they were no longer just little Eddie LeBaron and a wing and a prayer. First they added Don Meredith, who, after taking a blistering beating in his early days, learned to read defenses and perform in the precision manner demanded by Cowboy coach Tom Landry, one of the great coaches of all time. For Landry was a perfectionist who ran a very disciplined team. Either you did it his way or it was the highway.

He played offense a certain way and he played defense a certain way. And he tried to find players who could follow his dictates and fit his mold. Soon the Cowboys began to amass those quality ballplayers, like Bob Hayes and Don Perkins, along with the most talented individual at each position.

But it wasn't just outstanding talent that made the Cowboys a potentially great team. It was the coaching as well. Under Landry, the Cowboys installed a multiple set with a lot of motion on every play, making for a devastating offense. Add to that their Flex defense—with tackles on the weak side and backs off the ball, all the better to stop the run while also playing the pass—and you had the makings of a championship team.

Practicing against them every day, all day long, developed into a rivalry. And a dislike, even a "hate" for them.

Now here, folks, let me stop to explain *dislike* and *hate*. We're not talking about the hate that some groups in this country perpetuate on other people. We're talking about competitive hate.

Pro football was always very special for me, Deacon Jones. I was proud of my accomplishments and of my team and of my teammates. So the hate I'm talking about is a competitive hate, a dislike for the enemy in the field of battle. I disliked or hated anybody and everybody who wasn't on my team. Not a dislike or hate in the sense that I didn't respect these men on the other side of the ball. I respected them, their abilities, and their manhood. But as far as competition was concerned, I disliked—no, make that *hated*—anyone who had on a different-colored jersey than Deacon. I tried to deal with them all on an equal basis, to dish out pain and punishment to anybody in different uniform. It was the hate of actually performing, the hate of trying to become the best that day. I wanted to make everyone across the line of scrimmage feel just how I felt—and that was miserable. And while, as I have said, I had total respect for them, I wanted to take on all of them, head-on.

All opposing teams are created equal on the Deacon Jones "hate meter." But I guess I've always hated the Cowboys a little bit more. Why? Well, because they took a football and anointed themselves America's Team. To me, the only team worthy of that title is the world championship team, because the world champions stand alone above the pack. They've gone out there and hit somebody, knocked the hell out of somebody, and won the championship. You can't be self-appointed, you've got to earn it. I mean, how did they elect themselves America's Team? They probably held a secret vote down there in Dallas; the only team on the ballot was the Cowboys, and the only people allowed to vote were Dallas fans. How else could they get away with calling themselves America's Team? That didn't sit too well with me, back there in the Sixties. Or with anybody else on any other team at the time, for that matter. Maybe that's why the Cowboys were hated across the board.

Another reason I think a lot of people hate the Cowboys is that they have always had great talent, have always been a winner. This is a team that has always strived to be the best, has always met every challenge, and tried to put a winner on the field every year. They have done a great job of that, drafting well and getting great, productive players. But, let's face it, when you are always a winner, you are looked upon as the big bully on the block and everybody wants to take a shot at you, to knock you off your pedestal.

I also had a special reason: their management. Sure, the Cowboys had been one of the first teams to give players from small black colleges a chance to play back in those days. But over the years, their general manager, Tex Schramm, made several negative comments about our inability to serve in an administrative capacity. I found that very strange coming from a man who had done so much to get blacks into the game in the early days. I guess we were good only down on the field, not up in the front office. Nevertheless, the black players around the league did not take kindly to his comments, and that was one more nail in the Cowboys' coffin, one more reason to take your game to a greater level when you played them. It inspired us to greater heights because we disliked their management. And it furthered our "hate" of the Cowboys.

However, I never fully understood how much the Cowboys were disliked or hated until 1966. That was the year George Allen took over as head coach of the Los Angeles Rams.

Allen was a breath of fresh air. His schoolboyish enthusiasm and gung-ho spirit—complete with handmade motivational signs and endless pep talks—carried over to the entire team, instilling us with a winning attitude, something we hadn't had in many a season. His arrival was also accompanied by the gale-force winds of change. For now we had the largest playbook in the history of footballkind, drills, drills, and more drills—all, he said, to perfect our moves and our timing—and all-new training facilities at Cal State Fullerton.

Now we were just fifty miles or so, up the 101 Freeway, from the Cowboys' training camp in Thousand Oaks. And Allen challenged the Cowboys to a couple of practice sessions "to find out whether Tom's [Cowboy coach Tom Landry's] playbook is any better than mine."

Did I say "practice"? All-out war would be more like it. For some reason I couldn't understand then—and don't to this day—Allen and Landry didn't like each other. And it showed. Before every "practice" session against the Cowboys, George would address the team— more a pep talk than an address—filling us with his dislike for our "enemy," the Cowboys. Then, filled with his emotional fervor, we would almost tear down the door of the dressing room to get at *our* "enemy," willing to dedicate body and soul to beating—and beating up on— the Cowboys.

All of a sudden, those scrimmages that had once been leisurely run-throughs against a team considered to be just another NFL club became instead World War III. It was our front line against their front line, all day long, in full-contact exercises. First we would have the running game, then the passing game, and then the kicking game. That's the way it broke out, first team versus first team—no rookies need apply, thank you. And we would go at it, in half-field scrimmages, no holds barred, no questions asked.

If you remember those front lines—the Rams' "Fearsome Foursome" and the Cowboys' "Doomsday Defense," two of the most devastating defensive units in the history of pro football—it made for some of the most awesome scrimmages in NFL history. Every scrimmage was pure trench warfare, gladiator style; a preseason championship game.

We were to carry that rivalry and hatred on into the regular season, playing the Cowboys twice in the next four years—beating them 35–13 in 1967 and 24–23 in 1969, seasons in which both teams finished atop their respective divisions. And then, after the 1970 season, George Allen was gone, leaving Los Angeles to coach the Washington Redskins. And, for the moment, so too was my hatred for the Dallas Cowboys.

That hate was to rekindle in 1974 when I joined the Washington Redskins. And rejoined George Allen.

Here, let me take a brief time out to tell you how Deacon Jones came to be reunited with George Allen. I first came to the Rams in 1961 as their fourteenth-round draft choice out of tiny South Carolina State College. Over the next ten years, I had the pleasure of playing alongside Lamar Lundy, Rosey Grier, and Merlin Olsen on a front line that became celebrated as the Fearsome Foursome, and I was also honored by being selected to play in eight Pro Bowls and being named to the NFC Western All-Pro team seven times. However, with the departure of Allen, we inherited longtime UCLA coach Tommy Prothro. Tommy and I didn't get along, his theory of professional football being a little different from mine. In Prothro's first year, 1971, the Rams not only traded away most of their veteran players—players like Diron Talbert, Jack Pardee, Myron Pottios, Maxie Baughan, Richie Petitbon, and Tommy Mason—but also lost several games we shouldn't have, some because of amateurish coaching, including one to the Cowboys. The next year, as one book of the time wrote, "Prothro daringly traded off Deacon Jones," and I journeyed down the San Diego Freeway to join the San Diego Chargers. Now on the downside of my career, I played two seasons with a lightning bolt on the side of my helmet, playing in all fourteen games both seasons and making the Pro Bowl once. Then, in 1974, the coach, Harland Svare, was fired and replaced by guess who? That's right, Tommy Prothro. And for a second time, Prothro traded me, this time to the Washington Redskins, where I joined up with George Allen again, just in time for the 1974 season.

I thought I had already seen everything there was to see in Cowboy-hating. But I hadn't seen anything till I came to Washington. There I found out how much the Cowboys *really* were hated. It was a whole new level of Cowboy-hating and Cowboy-bashing—not just by the players, but by the entire community. This was Redskin territory, and everybody—and I mean *everybody*—hated the Cowboys.

The chief Cowboy-hater was, naturally, the chief of the Redskins, George Allen. His hatred of the Cowboys motivated his every move, moves directed at building a team that could challenge the Cowboys' domination of the NFC East. Because George's system was so complicated, he wanted players who could execute his system and not make mistakes. And so he began collecting veterans—a group of rejects, misfits, and malcontents he called the "Over the Hill Gang." The birth of the "Over the Hill Gang" brought together players who probably never could have existed in the league as individuals, but who were a formidable group collectively: Talbert, McDole, Hanburger, Kilmer, Pardee, Pottios, Owens,

Hauss, Jurgensen, Biggs, Brown, Taylor. If you ever had to go to war, these were the guys you'd want on your side. I was proud to be a part of that unit and even prouder to be able to take my "hate" for the Dallas Cowboys to another level.

Together we believed in two things: giving it our all, playing as hard and as tough as we possibly could; and living to play against the Dallas Cowboys.

Washington versus Dallas Week . . . This was the time of the year when fans hated Dallas even more than the players did. I would have been frightened if I had been a Cowboy and come into Redskin territory that week. These fans were serious. And believe me, ladies and gentlemen, everyone gets involved in Dallas Week—the President, the House of Representatives, the Senate, every politician worth his or her bill, every lobbyist. Everyone gets behind their beloved 'Skins. And everyone is a Cowboy-hater.

The two games in 1974 were brutal battles, two of the most emotional games I've ever played in. We won the first one in Washington, 28–21, but it wasn't easy. After we jumped out to a 28–0 halftime lead, the Cowboys came back to narrow the score to 28–21 in the fourth quarter. It took an interception by Mike Bass on our 3-yard line to halt one last-quarter drive and then our stopping them for four plays on the Redskins' 7-yard line in the final minute to seal the victory.

Two weeks later, down in Dallas on Thanksgiving Day, we played the second of our games against the Cowboys. And this one was more emotional than the first, if that were possible. The Redskins had gone ahead, 16–3, in the third quarter, but the Cowboys' rookie quarterback, Clint Longley—who had just come in to replace Roger Staubach, who had gone out with a concussion—

brought them back for two scores. After three, Dallas led, 17–16. But Billy Kilmer was equal to the task, driving the 'Skins downfield, where another Over the Hill reject, Duane Thomas, scored on a 19-yard run to put us back ahead, 23–17. Then, with just twenty-eight seconds left in the game, Longley, eluding a pass rush by Talbert and yours truly, unleashed a 50-yard Hail Mary pass somewhere in the direction of Drew Pearson. Pearson, despite being sandwiched between several Redskin defenders, made one heckuva catch for the winning touchdown.

You know, sometimes you just get to wondering if the Old Man upstairs is on your side because of some of the bounces that have gone Dallas's way. But Longley threw it and Pearson caught it, and that's what counts. Guess you've just got to hate the Cowboys for all four quarters, right up to the final gun. Anything short of that ain't enough.

After that emotionally charged season, I retired, certain that in fourteen seasons I had done everything and seen everything I wanted to.

Six years later Deacon Jones was inducted into the Pro Football Hall of Fame in Canton, Ohio. Ironically, two of the members of my Class of 1980 were members of the Dallas Cowboys, Bob Lilly and Herb Adderley, two of the greatest players in NFL history. I'm proud to call them my friends, along with other gentlemen who have played on the Cowboys, like Roger Staubach, Bob Hayes, and Rayfield Wright. For, as I said earlier, Deacon appreciates the competitiveness of the game, and while I may "hate" anyone across the line from me, I can still respect him for his abilities. And these men certainly have earned my respect for their achievements, even if they were Dallas Cowboys.

But if I respected the Cowboys of old, I find it difficult, if not impossible, to respect the Dallas Cowboys of today. It seems as if so many of the new breed on the Cowboys have no respect for what took place before they came on the scene and have thrown that America's Team thing right into the toilet.

They have no idea of what we went through back in my day, what we had to endure. Most of us back then, B.C.—Before the Civil Rights Movement—had an independent spirit and we paid for it. I know I did. We had to fight for everything they now take for granted.

We had to deal with speculation, common among sportswriters and league officials alike, on how many black faces were too many for one team. We had to deal with the pernicious practice of "stacking," having an even number of blacks, whether it be two, four, six, or eight, on one team so that we roomed together, never with a white teammate—a practice Vince Lombardi changed when he had Jerry Kramer room with Willie Davis. But then again, Lombardi treated all men equally: like dogs. And we had to deal with out-and-out discrimination, whether it be in the South or on the West Coast.

Today, those players who are our descendants have no knowledge of what went on before them. And have no incentive to research it, to learn it.

As Hank Aaron said of today's black baseball players, disappointed that so few had any knowledge of their own history, not even knowing who Jackie Robinson was or what he meant: "I'm sure Jackie would be proud of all the money they're making. But I suspect he'd want to shake some of them until the dollar signs fell from their eyes so they could once again see straight."

Like Hank, I also want to shake some of them—like Michael Irvin, Deion Sanders, Leon Lett, and Erik Williams—to make them appreciate what we went through and what they've inherited. To shake the greed out of them. To restore some of the guiding principles that motivated us back in the old days.

Today's players owe a responsibility to their team, their sport, and to society as a whole. But they have none. They have no social conscience, no scruples, no sense of self-sacrifice. Today's players have no team camaraderie, not wanting to put their bodies on the line for their fellow players. Their collective mission is one of "me . . . me . . . me . . . ," and when they speak, it's not out of pride, but out of a need to call attention to themselves.

No, I don't hate the Dallas Cowboys of today. I pity them. At least that's the view of Deacon Jones.

BILLY KILMER

MAYBE I MISSED SOMETHING, but I could never quite understand why the Dallas Cowboys called themselves America's Team. Nor, for that matter, why anyone else did.

When I toured Korea back in 1973 with a group of NFL players, all that anyone—officers, noncoms, everyone at the bases—wanted to talk about was the Redskins. Not the Cowboys. And almost every congressman and senator, no matter what part of the country he came from, rooted for the Redskins. Even Presidents.

Lyndon Johnson, a Texan down to his cowboy boots, could be found almost every Sunday in the owner's box, rooting for the Redskins—even against the Cowboys. And Richard Nixon did more than just root, he actually became involved, calling coach George Allen every Monday to discuss what strategy we had used in the game the day before or what strategy we were going to use in the upcoming Sunday game. Sometimes he even suggested a few plays of his own.

One of those plays came in the playoff game against

BILLY KILMER was a quarterback for the San Francisco 49ers, the New Orleans Saints, and the Washington Redskins in 1961, '62, '64, and from 1966 through 1978.

the San Francisco 49ers after the 1971 season. All week long we had practiced a reverse, a play I thought we might use somewhere in the middle of the field, outside the 30-yard lines, if the opportunity ever arose. Well, the opportunity did arise, but not when or how I expected it. We were ahead of the Niners 10–3, and driving for a score that would have given us a commanding fourteen-point lead. Now, I always called my own plays, but with the ball inside San Francisco's 10-yard line, a play came in from the bench: Run the reverse. I thought it was, at best, an unusual call. But I wasn't about to argue with a play that had been sent in by Coach Allen. So we ran it, and naturally it was stuffed by the 49ers' defense for a loss of six or seven yards. We never scored on that possession and would ultimately lose the game by four points. On the plane ride back to Washington, I went over to Coach Allen and asked him, "Where the dickens did *that* play come from?" Or words to that effect. Allen's answer was, "President Nixon gave us that play." I thought he was joking. But then again, Allen rarely joked about things like that.

Back to the subject at hand: Do I "hate" the Dallas Cowboys? I had some good friends on the Cowboys and could hate them only as you would hate a natural rival, much as I did USC when I played for UCLA, sort of a hate with a lowercased *h*. But George Allen hated them with a capital *H*. His antipathy toward the Cowboys was evident from his very first meeting with the Redskins as the new coach in 1971 and carried through every meeting and practice thereafter. He continually stressed that if the 'Skins were going to compete in the division and win a title, we had to beat the Cowboys. Everything he ever did or said was underscored with one message: Cowboys . . . Cowboys . . . Cowboys . . . over and over again, almost like a mantra.

The Cowboys had not always been the Redskins' rival. That didn't happen until George Allen came along. For the first few years of their existence, the Cowboys had been an expansion team, one that lost more games than it won. But, using owner Clint Murchison's money, they began to build their team through the draft and by the mid-1960s had put together one of the top teams in the league.

They also built one of the best off-the-field teams as well, a front office team of Tex Schramm and Gil Brandt. Together they would shape the Cowboys through astute marketing and promotion. And, not incidentally, a great scouting system.

Let me give you an example: Every year the NCAA coaches used to hold their convention in Dallas. And every year Tex and Gil would host the coaches, holding cocktail parties, barbecue parties, and golf tournaments for the visiting coaches, even going so far as to give them little presents, compliments of the Cowboys. Their planting harvested a lot of goodwill and a little Cowboy network among the college coaches, enabling Schramm and Brandt to call on the coaches for information that would help the Cowboys drafting players. It helped them in drafting Cornell Green, a basketball player nobody thought could play football, with a late-round draft choice. Ditto Pete Gent. And it helped them draft Bob Hayes, an Olympic track star, after Schramm and Brandt went down to Florida A&M to see his coach, Jake Gaithers, to ensure that Hayes would not jump to the rival American Football League.

So by the late 1960s, using power and money, the Cowboys had become one of the dominant franchises in the league and by far the dominant team in the NFC East. And then in 1971, enter George Allen as coach of the Washington Redskins, and all of a sudden Dallas had competition for the top spot in the division. And a rival.

Starting with that 1971 season, you knew that when the Redskins played the Cowboys, it would be more than a football game—it would be a war. And before every one of those games, Coach Allen would fire us up. Several times he would get up in front of the entire squad and say, "If it were up to me, I'd go toe-to-toe with Tom Landry on the fifty-yard line to decide the game."

Another time, I think it was sometime during the 1974 season, Allen walked into the meeting room in a kimono, followed by two Koreans holding plywood boards. Now, you know most team meetings: Half the players are asleep, and the other half wishes they were. But when we saw this out-of-the-ordinary scene in front of us, we all sat up and took notice, almost like we were saying in unison, "What the hell's going on here?" Standing in front of the entire Redskins team, Allen went through his "If it were up to me, I'd go toe-to-toe with Tom Landry on the fifty-yard line to decide the game" speech. And with that, he cracked one of the two plywood boards with his fist. Then he turned around and said, "And I'd do this to him right in the stomach," and side-kicked the other board in two. I never saw so much emotion in one room. Hell, after that Rockne-like speech, we could have gone out and whipped the Cowboys right then and there.

George was also not above using some psychology on the Cowboys. Especially when they came into RFK to play us. Back in 1971–1972, the Cowboys would come to the stadium on Saturday afternoons to practice. And so George would send our scouts out on the field dressed like yard workers and have them sweeping up the place while they scouted the Cowboys. He also had our equipment man dress up as a caretaker, complete with broom in hand, and go down on the field to help scout the 'Boys.

Another method of psychological warfare George practiced was telling the equipment man not to give the Cowboys any hot water in their locker room after practices. We heard that Landry and the team were more heated than the water over their ice-cold showers.

Landry soon developed a phobia about Allen, and instead of bringing the Cowboys in early in the week and working out at RFK, he would keep them home to practice and then come in the day before the game. But even in Dallas, Landry so spooked by Allen's every move, kept looking over his shoulder for George. To ensure that Allen couldn't place his scouts in the motel overlooking the Cowboys' practice field, Landry would rent out all the rooms on that side for the whole week. George, alone, was building the rivalry between the Redskins and the Cowboys.

When George came over to the Redskins from the Rams in 1971, he took over a team that had a pretty good offense, with Sonny Jurgensen, Larry Brown, Charley Taylor, and a good offensive line. However, the Redskins needed help on the defensive side of the ball, having given up 314 points in 1970—an average of more than twenty-two points a game. Operating under the philosophy that "The Future Is Now," George immediately set out to trade for veteran players. The resulting collection of football old-timers he accumulated from other teams—whether through free agency or trades (usually with draft choices)—included Diron Talbert, Myron Pottios, John Wilbur, and Richie Petitbon from the Rams; Ron McDole from the Bills; Verlon Biggs from the Jets; Clifton McNeil from the Giants; Roy Jefferson from the

Colts; Speedy Duncan from the Chargers; and, of course, yours truly from the Saints.

I was the first acquistion he made when he became coach of the 'Skins, trading the Saints linebacker Tom Roussel and Washington's fourth- and eighth-round choices in the 1971 draft for me. I can only remember that I didn't care for the trade. Not at all. I was then thirty-two years old and didn't have too many years left to play. I figured, Man, I'm never going to play ahead of Sonny. So I called Allen, saying something like "George, I appreciate your trading for me, but I want to play somewhere else, somewhere where I know I can play. And I know of two or three other teams that want my services, and I know I can play for them." But George didn't even hear what I said, instead launching into a "Look, Billy, I want you to come up here. I want to talk to you." I was so taken aback by his fast-talking that I could only say okay and flew up to Washington in late January, coincidentally the day of the 1971 draft. That was the day George pulled off the big trade with the team he called the "Ramskins," giving the Rams the Redskins' first and third choices in the 1971 draft, their third, fourth, fifth, sixth, and seventh choices in the 1972 draft, and linebacker Marlin McKeever for Diron Talbert, John Wilbur, Myron Pottios, Jack Pardee, and Maxie Baughan. Then he looked at me and said, "See this trade I made? We're going to be a winner here, and you're going to be part of it. We're going to go out and get the best players available, and we're going to win." I had been in the league for ten years and had never heard a coach talk like that.

With enthusiasm like that, how could I say no? And so I decided to play for the Redskins, but for only one year—never signing a contract, and playing out my option. But somehow, some way, everything fell into place for me. Sonny got hurt in a preseason exhibition game against Miami and was out for most of the year, so I got a chance to start and took the Redskins to the playoffs—the first time in twenty-six years for the 'Skins.

Come April 30 the next year, I still hadn't signed my contract with the Redskins. Now, in those days, May 1 was the deadline for signing contracts before a player became a free agent, and I was already talking to a couple of teams that wanted me for the upcoming season. And wouldn't you know it, George found me somehow while I was down in Florida fishing on April 30. He said, "Billy, you've got to come up here. I've got to talk to you. We gotta have you, you can't go anywhere else." By the next day I was up in Washington, and George and I worked out a contract that was, even by reflection, pretty good for me. Back then I was only making $30,000 a year, and George not only jumped me up considerably but gave me a bonus to reward me for 1971. I was now "officially" a Redskin, a member of the family. And a rival of the Dallas Cowboys.

I played many games against the Cowboys—seventeen, to be exact—and playing against them was always a thrill. I guess the best game I ever played against them was for the 1972 NFC championship. We had played them twice during the regular season and, like most years, had split the series, winning in Washington and losing down in Dallas. Still, we finished a game ahead of them in the NFC East—the first time they had been displaced as champions since 1966—and now were facing them a third time for the NFC title and the right to go to the Super Bowl.

On the morning of the game, I met with my usual pregame coffee klatch, a group that included Diron Talbert,

Lenny Hauss, and Ron McDole. All week long I had been tense, unable to sleep and edgy about the game. After all, this was my first chance to go to the big one, the Super Bowl. As I came into the Marriott hotel coffee shop the morning of the game, one of the guys threw me a copy of that morning's paper and said, "Here, read this article," pointing to something on the front page. And there it was, in black-and-white, Tom Landry saying that the Cowboys would beat the Redskins and then going on to say, "The reason why I say we'll beat the Redskins is one thing, and that's because Roger Staubach is a better athlete than Billy Kilmer."

I saw red, not the burgundy red worn by the Redskins, but hot red, as in rage. I mean, Roger is a fine athlete and all that, but I had been an All-American basketball player in high school and had a basketball scholarship to UCLA. Plus, I could have signed a contract for $50,000 to play baseball right out of high school. To say nothing of my football exploits. That was it. I was going to show Landry and the world that I was the better athlete on this afternoon of all afternoons.

And I did. You can look it up: I completed 14 of 18 passes for two touchdowns and 194 yards, while Staubach had only 9 completions in 20 attempts for no touchdowns. Hell, I even ran for 15 yards as we beat the Cowboys, 28–3, for the NFC championship.

I had another memorable game against the Cowboys in 1975 at RFK Stadium. As an aside, I was very friendly with Cowboys owners Clint Murchison and Bedford Wynne. They always came into Washington on a Friday, and I'd spend a little time with them, sort of consorting with the enemy, if you will. Well, I had what might charitably be called a bad game that Sunday, throwing four interceptions. And the hometown crowd was on me pretty good, booing my every move. My fourth interception went to Cliff Harris, probably the only interception he ever made in his career, and he ran it in for the go-ahead touchdown, making the score 23–16, Dallas, with just over two minutes left. We got the ball back on the kickoff, and with the crowd booing, I drove the team downfield, hitting Jerry Smith in the end zone to tie the score at 23.

When their kicker, Toni Fritsch, missed a 38-yard field goal attempt with five seconds left in regulation, the game went into overtime. However, he had nothing on our kicker, Mark Moseley, who had missed three field goals earlier in the game. Well, Dallas won the coin toss, and Staubach started moving the Cowboys down the field. But then, just as they seemed to be moving the ball into field goal range, Kenny Houston stepped in front of a Dallas receiver to pick off a Staubach pass and returned it to midfield. Add a 15-yard personal foul penalty against one of those mean ol' Cowboys and we now had the ball on their 35. We drove down to the 20, within field-goal range, and I had an idea that Allen wanted me to run the ball up the middle to set up the potential game-winning field goal. Hell, I wasn't going to have any of that. In the huddle I crouched down and said, "Look, guys, we're not going to let the kicker lose the game for us. We're going to score a touchdown." And with that, I called a play-action pass and threw to Charley Taylor close to the first-down marker.

As I walked over to where the officials were measuring to see if we had the first down, Bedford Wynne, who was down on the Dallas bench, came running over to the sidelines shouting, over and over again, "Do it . . . do it . . . kick a field goal . . . kick a field goal . . . you've won the game." I knew he had bet on the Cowboys, as he always did no matter where or who they played, and probably had gotten three and a half points, so I looked at him and said, "Screw you, Bedford, we're scoring a touchdown." On the next play we drove to the one-foot line, and then I dove the one foot for the touchdown that won the game. It was a sweet victory, made all the sweeter by the fact that I had beaten our rivals, the Cowboys, and cost one of their owners some money besides.

Now let me go back and fill you in on a little history, something that may give you an idea why the Redskins, under George Allen, and the Dallas Cowboys became "hated"—there's that word—archrivals. George always thought that Pete Rozelle and Tex Schramm kind of ran the league in those days. The two had been buddies when they both worked for the Los Angeles Rams back in the 1950s, and Tex had helped Pete get the commissioner's job in 1960. So the connection went back a long way. And George knew it. And he always felt, rightly or wrongly, that Tex and Pete were plotting against the Redskins. And, conversely, for the Cowboys.

Plotting for the Cowboys always seemed to be a natural way of doing business. One incident illustrates the power Tex Schramm exerted in the league: the 1977 draft. At the time, the Seattle Seahawks were a new team, an expansion team, newly minted in 1976. By virtue of their first-year 2–12 record, they had "earned" the rights to the second choice in the 1977 draft. At the time, the best prospect in the country was Tony Dorsett, who had just won the Heisman Trophy. Obviously, the Seahawks were interested in Dorsett. He was a player they could build their team around, a so-called franchise player. Well, I was in Dallas on the day of the draft and couldn't believe what I heard, which was that the Seattle director of player personnel, Dick Mansperger (who just happened to have worked for Schramm and the Cowboys before he went to Seattle and who owed an allegiance to Schramm), had—wouldn't you know it?—traded Seattle's first-round draft choice (which turned out to be Dorsett) for Dallas's first-round choice, fourteenth in the draft overall, and two second-round picks. And nobody, but nobody, said a word. Nobody, that is, except George Allen, who was very upset. The trade was to him, and to anyone else who analyzed it, merely another example of Cowboy power. And arrogance.

George, you see, didn't give two hoots and a holler about draft choices. When a free agent like John Riggins or Calvin Hill became available, George would go after him. He gave the New York Jets two number-one draft choices for Riggins (who therefore became his number-one draft pick). Calvin was a free agent who had jumped to the World Football League and then come back. Dallas thought it had the rights to him. But George picked him up without any compensation to Dallas, and Commissioner Rozelle was upset because, back in those days, the so-called Rozelle Rule was in effect: a team signing a player from another team had to give that former team two number-one draft choices. And Rozelle felt that Allen had ridiculed him and his rule. But George didn't care about draft choices. He'd give up any of them—even if he didn't have them, once trading the same draft choice to two different teams—to get the players he needed to win.

A few years before, he had gotten Dave Butz, who was playing out his option with the St. Louis Cardinals, by giving the Cardinals two number-one draft choices. He was raiding the rest of the league, and I think that Schramm, who believed in building through the draft, disliked George's way of doing business. Everybody else in the league complied with Schramm's dictates, but not Allen. George was a maverick.

I believe that the Cowboys got their pound's worth of flesh in 1978 when George, after being fired by the Redskins following the 1977 season, returned to the Rams as head coach and lasted all of two exhibition games. Out of work, he tried mightily to latch on with another team. But nobody would hire him. Although I don't have proof of this, I firmly believe George was blackballed by the league. George and I discussed this at length several times, and he was convinced that the Cowboys somewhere had their hand in his inability to get another job in the NFL.

Over the years I have had the pleasure of consorting with "the enemy," former members of the Cowboys. It's something similar to liking your former in-laws. But being friendly with guys like Bob Lilly, Roger Staubach, and Lee Roy Jordan, you'd always find yourself on mutual ground talking about Tex Schramm—and the discussion would always get around to how stingy he was. These guys were All-Pros and never got paid what they were worth. I made more than Roger and could never understand it. I was always amazed that even when Roger took the Cowboys to Super Bowl wins, he was still paid less than Joe Namath and several other quarterbacks in the league.

One of the ploys Schramm used when players came in to negotiate contracts would be to add up all their playoff money and the money they made from the Cowboys' speakers' bureau and off-season personal appearances and then say, "See what you got just for being a Cowboy." Or "You made a healthy salary; you're above the average of everybody in the league." I never thought that was fair. They should have been compensated first, and the rest would have been gravy, gravy they earned by being winners. But Tex never saw it that way.

So, you see, it wasn't just the Redskins or the Eagles or the Giants or the Cardinals who didn't like the Cowboys. Hell, even some of the Cowboys didn't like the Cowboys. But "hate" the Cowboys? Well, George Allen did. And that's good enough for me.

JERRY KRAMER

THE DALLAS COWBOYS MAY call themselves America's Team, but calling yourself something doesn't make it so. Not by a long shot.

Remember that Smith Barney commercial in which John Houseman said, "We make the money the old-fashioned way . . . we earn it"? Well, you've got to earn a title like America's Team, not just claim it. And then wear it with the old-fashioned respect it deserves.

Being a professional football player has always been something very special to me. When I first began playing for the Green Bay Packers back in 1958, a lot of guys in the league chewed tobacco and, to tell you the truth, weren't very professional, either in appearance or attitude. As a matter of fact, professional football wasn't really all that professional then, either. The first television contract back then was somewhere in the neighborhood of $250,000—it certainly wasn't a great deal more than that. But Vince Lombardi impressed upon us

---

JERRY KRAMER, a member of the NFL's "All-Decade" Team for the Sixties, was an offensive guard for the Green Bay Packers from 1958 through 1968. He is the author of two books, Instant Replay *and* Distant Replay.

that we had to bring a degree of class, a degree of professionalism to the game. He would hold America's great corporations—IBM, General Motors, etc.—up as an example to us, telling us we had to perform like they did. And the Packers took it upon ourselves to represent pro football in a positive manner. So much so that, in the end, the great corporations were holding *us* up as an example—in preparation, commitment, and discipline.

I guess that's why I've always been sensitive to anything that detracts from what we tried to do in raising the image of the pro football player. I remember, back about the time I retired, O. J. Simpson doing an RC Cola commercial. He picked up the bottle of RC and tilted it back to drink it. Then someone, off camera, said something to him and he looked away without putting the bottle down, and the cola just ran down the front of his jersey. And I thought to myself, Here we go again. We had worked so hard to overcome the image of football players: that if you were big, then you were automatically stupid, and if you were a really big jock, then you were *really* stupid.

Throughout the intervening years I have had occasion to be proud of several ex-NFLers—like Alex Karras and Merlin Olsen, who went to Hollywood and succeeded in a very different and difficult environment. They used intelligence and emotional maturity to compete and excel in the outside world. But I continue to be sensitive to the image of the professional football player, and to anything that undermines all the hard work of so many to overcome the image of our being dumb jocks.

That's why I hate the Dallas Cowboys of today. After all those years of an attempting to shed the "dumb jock" image, here they are, down on the field acting like fools and reinforcing the image so many of us have tried so hard to change. All those years of working hard to re-make our image destroyed in a few taunting seconds. And every time I see them dancing and prancing around, conducting themselves like idiots, I'm embarrassed for them—and for all my fellow football players.

The Cowboys of yesteryear—the Tom Landry Cow-boys of Don Meredith, Bob Lilly, George Andrie, Lee Roy Jordan, Roger Staubach, Jethro Pugh, and Calvin Hill—were a wonderful group, one possessing quality and dig-nity. And as such, they represented the true virtues of the cowboy in our culture, the ones we became familiar with every time we saw John Wayne up there on the screen portraying one with his quiet, strong honesty, his integrity, his pride, his selflessness, and all the other attributes of the hardworking cowboy.

Today a few, a very few, of the current crop of Cow-boys possess those same attributes—players like Troy Aikman (who is my daughter Alicia's all-time favorite player), Emmitt Smith, Jay Novacek, and Daryl "Moose" Johnston. But, unfortunately, they are trapped in a sit-uation they can't control and have to endure most of the rest of their teammates playing with an arrogant, egotis-tical "me-ism" that demeans the entire club and de-means everyone who went before them. It's an attitude I can't stand. It's easy to see why a bunch of surly; strut-ting, swaggering players call themselves America's Team. But I can't understand anyone else doing it.

However, there is one team, now and forever, that re-flects America's virtues and is worthy of the title Amer-ica's Team: the Green Bay Packers.

The Packers are the classic American team, the only original franchise left over from the NFL's very first year, 1920, their name coming from the local packing com-pany that underwrote Curly Lambeau's dream of having a professional football team in the classic American town, Green Bay, Wisconsin. Over the succeeding years, the Packers have been a friendly, community-owned, family-oriented organization, one that has reflected its own community's values and America's as well.

When I say America's values, I mean the ones America grew up with, back when our uncle lived across the street, our grandparents three blocks away, and our parents across town. We were a family and were close with, and to, one another. However, we've now entered an era in which we have what they call a satellite family, one scattered to the four winds. And now those same family members, the uncle, the grandparents, and the parents, are in, say, Buffalo, Denver, and New Orleans. With very few people keeping their roots in the area they grew up in, we no longer have the traditional family units, or family identity. And while thousands upon thousands, even millions, may have abandoned their hometowns, they will never abandon their hometown team. It now becomes their identity, their link to the past, their extended family. And Green Bay, which reflects many of America's traditional values, has become, for many, their extended family.

But not only was the Green Bay franchise part of the family, so too were the Green Bay fans. They loved their Packers and watched out for us just like family. I recall, when I was playing, if a white Cadillac with a #5 license plate was out a little after curfew, Coach Lombardi would receive several phone calls letting him know where his Golden Boy, Paul Hornung, had parked his car—even when it moved and probably what time it was headed back to the dormitory. They kind of looked out for us. We were their team and we were part of their family.

When I go back to Green Bay, after having been away for almost thirty years, people come up to me on the street with friendly smiles, warm handshakes, and an amiable greeting or two, like "Hi, Jerry, how you doing?" Or "Hey, Jerry, how've you been?" And the one I like best, "Gee, Jerry, you're looking great. You haven't changed a bit." It's like going back to visit family.

Packer fans have always been the greatest in the world. And I guess you could say they represent the best of what pro football is all about. The one moment that sticks out in my mind as best illustrating that came on a fumble, of all things, *our* fumble—an odd way for fans to show what they're really all about. There we were, playing Baltimore in our next-to-last game of the 1968 season, our last home game. Going into the game we were still mathematically alive, but only if we won and almost everybody else lost—and then, I think, we would have had to carry out the computation to about the seventh decimal place. The short of it was that we needed the win badly. As the game wound down, we were two scores behind, but we had the ball with less than four minutes to go. We knew, in our heart of hearts, that we were going to march straight down the field and score, just as we always had. And sure enough, we began to move the ball downfield, bing, bang, bong, just as we had in years before. But then, just as our drive had moved us into scoring position, we fumbled and Baltimore recovered the ball. We knew it was over and so did the fifty thousand or more up in the stands. But as we trotted off Lambeau Field, heads held low, eliminated from any possibility of winning our fourth consecutive title, the fans rose as one in a spontaneous gesture to give us a five-minute ovation. It was almost as if they were saying, "It's over. We know it's over. But thank you for the wonderful memories, thank you for yesterday. Thank you for all you've done." It was truly one of the most memorable moments of my career and best epitomizes the emotional bond between the community of Green Bay, the state of Wisconsin, and the team.

It's a bond that has continued, long past our active association with the team. When I went down to New Orleans for the Super Bowl earlier this year, I had determined that I was just going to relax and enjoy the weekend with my friends and family. No autographs, no anything. This was not my day; it belonged to the Packers of 1996.

There were so many Packer fans down there, just walking down Bourbon Street was like walking around Lambeau Field. And almost every one of them came up to me and asked for my autograph. I'd wind up signing autographs for three or four hours, nonstop. You'd sign one, then you'd sign two, and before you knew it, you'd be doing it all night long. And as I looked into the faces of the people asking me for my autograph, it seemed they wanted something more. It was almost as if they needed to touch you, to get a piece of you, to somehow rise above their everyday lives and share something special with you. And then I understood what it was they really wanted. They wanted heroes. America needs heroes, needs role models, and these people were looking to me as one, albeit one from a long time ago.

Last season I had the opportunity to ask NFL Commissioner Paul Tagliabue something that has been bothering me for a long time. "Commissioner," I asked, "can you explain to me the relationship between a fan and a team?" And although the commissioner expressed some thoughts having to do with both sociological and psychological reasons, his reply, "Jerry, we've been pon-

dering that for a long time and we're really not sure . . . ,"
still left the question unanswered.

Maybe, just maybe, I thought, the answer might be
found in the statement of Charles Barkley, one of the
most outspoken athletes on the scene today, when he
said, "I'm no role model. Your mama and daddy should
be your role models." In a very real sense, he's absolutely correct. They should be the ones kids look up to.
But in reality, many times the kids look to athletes as
their role models. There's nothing we can do about it,
that's just the way it is. And you can only hope you conduct yourself with the class and the dignity of a Michael
Jordan or a Tiger Woods, two role models of today. Or
some of the wonderful athletes I was associated with,
players like Bart Starr and Carrol Dale and Willie Davis
and Bob Skoronski and on and on . . .

It's a hard thing to realize that you are actually a role
model for others or that in some way they have been
inspired by you. But I'd like to think the Packers of old
had the virtues that made us role models to an entire
generation of fans. The virtues we had were instilled in
us by Vincent Thomas Lombardi, our head coach, *the*
head coach. As young men, I guess we really couldn't
see beyond next week or the week after. But Lombardi
could see the gap between who we were then and what
we could become and felt it was his God-given responsibility to close that gap. And because he would not re-
lent in carrying out what he saw as his responsibility,
we all became his disciples, better men and, hopefully,
role models America could look up to.

I never really had given a great deal of thought to being
a role model until someone sent me a tape of an interview Tommy Lee Jones had done on the *Charlie Rose
Show* last year promoting his latest movie, *Cobb*. Rose

was exploring whether athletes served as role models
and asked Tommy Lee, "Does the athletic role model
work?" And Tommy Lee had answered, "Yes, it does,
absolutely. . . ." Asked why, Jones went on, "Well, it
teaches you discipline, commitment, preparation; it
teaches you so many things. . . ." Rose then asked, "Did
it work for you?" And Tommy Lee said, "Absolutely. I
always wanted to be Jerry Kramer. All my life I wanted
to be Jerry Kramer. I watched him for years and watched
every move he made. What I learned from him is of deep
and lasting value to me today." And I looked at this great
actor, one I have always admired for his roles in films
like *The Fugitive* and *Lonesome Dove,* and thought, Here
is a guy who had been an all–Ivy League lineman and he
had been inspired by me and my team. It was a great
feeling to know that you have had that effect on such a
great man.

And that's what we were, Bart Starr, Carrol Dale, Willie
Davis, Bob Skoronski, all of us . . . role models.

However, that was then. Now the torch has passed to
a whole new generation of athletes. Let me tell you
something that happened last year at the conference
championship game against Carolina. I was watching the
game with Bart Starr, Willie Davis, Ray Nitschke, and the
commissioner, plus a few others up in the box. And Bart
was sitting a few seats down the way, watching the game
intently. As you may remember, Brett Favre was having
a great day. Now, here was Green Bay's next great quarterback having a superb day on the field, and I was
watching Bart's reaction as he watched the man who
was taking his place as the next Green Bay quarterback
legend. And I wondered how Bart was feeling. Well, with
the game in hand, Favre came off the field to a standing
ovation. And I looked over and there was Bart, standing

and applauding the man who had succeeded him as a Packer institution. And I thought, What a mark of class. What a mark of dignity. What a special human being. And what a special group of players I was associated with.

But that's the Green Bay Packer team of today, a special group of players and great role models. There's Reggie White, a religious man and a great leader. There's Brett Favre, as pure and as decent a kid as you could find anywhere, unspoiled by success. And then there's Adam Timmerman, an articulate sweetheart of a kid, who, hearing of a farmer in Iowa who had cancer and never had the opportunity to attend a ballgame, arranged to have the farmer come to Green Bay, got him two tickets, and looked after him all weekend—even taking the farmer home for dinner. Adam didn't even know him, but he heard the guy was in trouble and having a tough time of it, so he stretched out his hand to help him. These are the virtues America can identify with, the virtues of a real America's Team. And role models America can be proud of.

Compare those virtues with the virtues of the Dallas Cowboys. Again, back to Charles Barkley, who was saying that "a lot of the young athletes of today are great role models if kids want to grow up to be a drug dealer or a pimp." Well, that's what I think of when I look at the Dallas Cowboys of today. There they are, strutting and swaggering around, giving off all the wrong signals for the kids of today.

This is not America's Team. This is more like America's children, trying to find out who they are, posturing and screaming and making asses of themselves in front of the TV cameras. Every time I see them on TV, I don't know whether to root for the defense or root for the prosecution. No, this will never be America's Team. If this is, then woe is America.

America needs real heroes, not players who call Dial-a-Prayer and ask for their own messages. Or players like Erik Williams, who came down on the back of defensive lineman John Jurkovic's leg and ended his career in Green Bay in as chickenshit a cheap shot as I've ever seen. I hate that. And I hate the Cowboys who play that way. That sort of stuff wouldn't play in Green Bay.

America's Team? Give me Green Bay any day. The Green Bay Packers have always been associated with pride, excellence, quality, dignity, discipline—all those wonderful qualities we have stood for over the years. That's why the Packers are America's *real* team, not the Cowboys. We've earned it, the old-fashioned way.

THOM LOVERRO

IT IS THE YEAR 2097. A youngster sits in front of his computer for a history lesson, part of his home schooling—now the way all students are taught. His father sits in the living room nearby, ordering dinner for the family that night via their interactive teleunit. His son comes into the room, taking a break from his lesson.

"All done with your history class, son?" the father asks.

"Yes, for now, Dad," the boy says. "It's all sort of confusing to me."

"Why, son?"

"Well, we're studying the fall of that country . . . you know . . . America?"

"Yes, son, I went to school, too, remember. I learned all about America in school as well. What can I help you with?" the father asks.

"What I don't understand is, this whole dispute over what really caused America to fall. They were once this world power, but what happened after that? I know

---

THOM LOVERRO is a sports columnist for the Washington Times *and is the author of* The Authorized History of the Washington Redskins.

there were civil wars and nuclear disasters, but one kid in class asked a question that caused a lot of trouble. In fact, they simply shut down the class for the day," the son says.

"What was the question, son?"

"This kid asked if it was true that what really caused the demise of America was something called the Dallas Cowboys," the boy says. "As soon as he asked it, the class was shut down. What were the Dallas Cowboys, Dad?"

The father suddenly looks very solemn. He calls his wife into the room.

"Billy here just asked what the Dallas Cowboys were," the man says to his wife. "What should I do?"

"I think you should tell him," the wife says. "Your father told you, and his father told him. Don't let him grow up believing the claptrap they teach in school about the great war and all that. Let him know the truth."

The son asks, "What is it, Dad? What were the Dallas Cowboys, and why is everyone so scared to talk about them?"

The father sits down on the couch. "Sit down next to me, son," he says. "This will take a while, and it may be a little confusing. But it's very important. It shaped events in the world for the last hundred years or so."

The son sits down with a frightened look on his face, as if he is going to hear a horror story.

"Don't be scared, son," the father says. "They can't hurt us anymore. But it's an important lesson, to make sure we don't make the same mistakes today. We can never have anything like the Dallas Cowboys happen again."

"Tell me, Dad," the boy says. "I can handle it."

"Well, now, this is the story as told to me by my father,

and as told to him. It's not written anywhere because of the laws forbidding any official acknowledgment of the existence of something called the Dallas Cowboys.

"Many years ago, they used to play professional football on the field, with real players, not like they do today, electronically with computer programs," the father says.

"As you know, they had to ban football-playing with humans when a number of players started to simply explode from steroid abuse," the father says. "But years ago, they used to play in stadiums in front of people, wearing all kinds of armor.

"More than a hundred years ago, around 1960 or so, the Dallas Cowboys were born," the father says. "They were a football team from a city called Dallas in a place called Texas in the country called America. That was the first problem. Everyone in Texas believed they were part of some legacy, you know, the wild frontier and all that, when it turned out that Texas was nothing more than one big gas and convenience store, and everyone living in it a glorified 7-Eleven clerk.

"So it was fertile ground for grandiose ideas, and somehow the idea that the Dallas Cowboys were America's Team was born. This didn't make sense, since there were more important teams in football, and certainly ones more worthy of a country's identity, but these Dallas Cowboys were an arrogant bunch and got everyone to go along with this premise, and they rose to power as America's Team.

"They were able to do this because they had a very influential leader, someone named Tom Landry. This was a cold, calculating individual who created this hypocritical image that his team was truly representative of America, and he even lent to the myth that he was

America's coach. . . . Actually, some people called him God's coach."

"Really, Dad?" the son asks. "This Coach Landry must have been a very charismatic leader."

"Actually, son, he had all the charm of a parking meter, but the man behind him really pulled the strings to foist this image of America's Team. According to the legend, it was this fellow named Tex Schramm who really set up the phony image of this wonderful football team and how it represented America. If the Dallas Cowboys represented America, then America was one big fraternity house, with drugs, booze, and women as their founding fathers."

"Tex? His name was really Tex?" the son asks incredulously.

"His real name might have been Pinkerton Smedley, given the baloney that used to come out of the Cowboys' image machine. This was America's Team, son. A quarterback named Dandy who wanted to be country-and-western singer more than a quarterback. Wide receivers named Golden who were anything but. A linebacker who called himself Hollywood, the originator of the chest-thumping flamboyant style that brought nothing but ruin to sports and society years later, a player who thought a coke spoon was part of his equipment. A group of exotic dancers called the Dallas Cowboys Cheerleaders who would have been arrested for dressing and dancing like they did in most of these Bible-thumping Texas towns but were worshiped within the confines of Texas Stadium. Hypocrisy! Hypocrisy! Why couldn't they see it?" The father's voice rises with anger. He slams his fist on the table.

"Dad, Dad, take it easy," the son says. "You're scaring me."

"I'm . . . I'm sorry son," the father says. "It's just that now it seems all so senseless. Why didn't people see through all of this? How could they embrace it?"

"Drugs?" the son asks.

"Maybe," the father says. "Maybe the whole nation was under the influence of something."

"Dad, didn't they also elect an actor who starred with a monkey in the movies as their President?" the son asks.

"True, son, you have a point," the father says. "But that doesn't make it any less frustrating."

"But, Dad, the same players didn't play for the Dallas Cowboys for all those years, right? This guy Landry didn't coach them for fifty years, did he?"

"You're right, son," the father says. "Landry wasn't the coach forever, though he probably thought he should have been. Eventually, the caliber of thugs the Cowboys had on their team weren't very talented football players, and America's Team started losing, so Landry and Schramm were no longer the high priests of the Cowboys' religion."

"Was Landry a religious man?" the son asks.

"He thought so, from what I've been told," the father says. "But he bought into being part of this good and wholesome Cowboy image, ignoring all the sins of his players for the sake of the Cowboys. Yeah, he was religious all right. He worshiped at the altar of football."

"But didn't all that end after Landry and Schramm were gone?" the son asks.

"You would have thought so, son, but that's perhaps what is so startling about this story. It's as if the Cowboys were destined to be America's curse, not America's Team. If you can believe it, things got worse."

"No," the son says. "How could that be? How could things get any worse?"

"Jerry Jones," the father says.

"Dad!" the son says, shocked. "You know the law. You know it's forbidden to speak that name!"

"Do you know why, son?"

"No," the son replies. "No one ever taught us why it is forbidden. We just learned that it is one of the worst things a person in our society could possibly say. No one ever told me why, and I guess as kids we've always been too scared to ask."

"I'll tell you why," the father says in hushed tones. "But you must promise not to tell anyone else, except to pass on the truth to your son someday.

"Jerry Jones was an oilman . . ." the father says.

"My gosh, that's bad enough," the son says.

"I know, but he wasn't satisfied with being just a prof-iteering weasel. He wanted more, and when the Cow-boys went up for sale, Jones bought the team. At first, it didn't seem like it would mean much; in fact, it ap-peared as if the reign of America's Team was over. Jones fired Tom Landry, and though he was vilified for it by many, it could have been an important moment in the history of civilization."

"Didn't that end the frightening reign of the Cowboys as America's Team, Dad?" the son asks.

"No, son. That's what's so disturbing. This fellow Jerry Jones was more troublesome than either Landry or Schramm. He wasn't as hypocritical, but he was far more power-hungry and obsessed with himself and his place in history. He got lucky and hired a football coach named Jimmy Johnson, and they made some moves that turned the Cowboys around quickly from losers to Su-per Bowl champions.

"But there wasn't enough room even in a place as big as Texas for these two egos, and they split up, even after winning two Super Bowls. Then this fellow Jones went out and hired the anti-Landry, or the Devil's coach, if you will, a man named Barry Switzer, who once ran a college football team that was more like a motorcycle gang than a group of student-athletes. This guy Switzer couldn't get a job coaching a fantasy football team, yet Jones, his good friend, hired him to coach America's Team."

"Why did he hire this Switzer fellow?" the son asks.

"Because, son, he turned out to be the perfect coach for this latest version of America's Team," the father says. "These players made those convicts he coached at that college look like Boy Scouts.

"This was a bunch of arrogant, trash-talking thugs who operated like they were immune from the rules of society. That was the benefit of being America's Team. They won on the field and did what they pleased off it, and though they received their share of criticism, they were still the biggest thing in sports. People couldn't get enough of the Dallas Cowboys, even though the news they got came from the courtroom as much as from the football field.

"They had a receiver named Michael Irvin, who wound up getting arrested for drugs. You won't believe this, but he got arrested in a motel room with some exotic dancers. Then a cop supposedly tried to have him killed because Irvin supposedly threatened the guy's girlfriend about her testimony to something called a grand jury about this secret place the Cowboys used to have their sex and drug parties. . . ."

The son sits there with his jaw open in disbelief. "This was America's Team?"

"Yes sir, son," the father says. "Maybe now you're getting an idea of what went wrong with America.

"This guy Irvin is getting arrested, and do you want

to know what he says to the cops? He says, 'Can I tell you who I am?' thinking that would get him out of trouble."

"But it didn't, right?" the son asks. "He went to jail, right? He wasn't a Cowboy anymore after that, was he?"

"Son, son, haven't you been listening?" the father asks. "When you play for America's Team, you don't go to jail. You get a vacation, then you come back and play again. He walked into court wearing a fur coat and acting like a rock star. He knew Cowboys didn't go to jail.

"And he was far from the only one. The Cowboys had so many players who were caught using drugs that people started jokingly calling them 'South America's Team.'

"Everybody thought the Cowboys would fall after that, but all it did was seem to enhance their attraction to America," the father says. "Large corporations, like a company called Nike, continued to pay large amounts of money just to be affiliated with the Cowboys."

"Nike?" the son asks. "Isn't that the company that wound up agreeing to pay part of America's deficit in return for letting them put that stupid swoosh mark on the country's currency?"

"Yes, son, the very same," the father says. "And, you see, that's what helped contribute to the downfall of America. A whole corporate society fed off the image of the Dallas Cowboys, from the time of Saint Tom to Barry the Bootlegger's Boy. The Cowboys set the standard for image in America, and those standards eventually fell so low that the country tore itself apart. No one believed they had to live by the rules. Everyone wanted to be like Michael Irvin, and those that didn't lived by the hypocrisy practiced by Landry, Schramm, and the previous keepers of the frightening flame. What really happened was that America became the Cowboys' country, not that the Cowboys became America's Team."

"Dad, this all sounds sort of far-fetched," the son says. "It's kind of hard to believe."

"Son, many people don't believe it," the father says. "I've had many people scoff at me, so much that I stopped talking about it. But my father told me to expect disbelievers. Son, you'll have to make up your own mind."

"Okay, Dad, let me think about it," the son says. "You've told me quite a story."

As the son walks out of the room, he calls back to his father, "Dad, you said your father told you about the Dallas Cowboys, and his father told him. Don't I remember you telling me once that they used to root for a professional football team called the Washington Redskins?"

"Yes, son, that's true," the father replies. "Why do you ask?"

"No reason," the son says, walking away smiling.

WALLACE MATTHEWS

CAN I TELL YOU who I am?

I am a man who hates the Dallas Cowboys the way Jerry Jones loves to lose. I am a man who hates the Dallas Cowboys the way Nate Newton hates doing sit-ups.

This is not a recent thing. I hated the Dallas Cowboys long before it was fashionable, long before they became America's Team and then America's Most Wanted Team.

For years, they have ruined my Thanksgiving dinner. Doesn't matter if they won or lost, just the sight of the blue star on my TV set was enough to transform the tenderest turkey into petrified wood, sour the sweetest cranberry sauce, turn the most succulent stuffing into sawdust.

My antipathy toward the Dallas Cowboys goes way, way back, to the days of Tom Landry and Tex Schramm and Dandy Don Meredith, the Lipton tea–loving quarterback with hay between his capped teeth.

These days, the names are different—Barry Switzer, Jerry Jones, Michael Irvin, Deion Sanders—but the song remains the same.

WALLACE MATTHEWS is a sports columnist for the New York Post.

Deep in the heart of Texas, something is terribly rotten.

I don't like the city of Dallas, I don't like the stadium—who thought it would be a good idea to cut that ridiculous askew hole in the ceiling anyway?—I'm not crazy about the uniforms, and I've always viewed J. R. Ewing as a pudgy rug-wearing fraud with cowshit on his boots.

Texans, of course, think J.R. is menacing, the same way they think Switzer is bright or Jones is shrewd.

But they are none of these things.

What they are, in a word, is crude—and I don't mean the kind that comes a-bubbling up from the Texas soil.

There is nothing oilier than Texas slick, nothing more sickening than Texas proud, nothing sadder than a whole city that lives and dies with the fortunes of a football team.

But then, what can you expect from a city that has a rivalry with Houston (of all places) and is still jealous over the fact that the first word from the surface of the moon was the name of its hated rival: "Houston, Tranquillity Base here" still chaps the ass of every self-respecting Dallasite because, let's face it, that's one more claim to fame Houston has over Dallas, which before the rise of the Cowboys didn't have any.

After all, in the pre–America's Team era, how must it have felt for Dallas to be known only for being unable to keep the President of the United States from being gunned down by a sniper in broad daylight, and then being unable to keep his accused killer from being gunned down in the basement of the police station on live TV?

No wonder one of the last sentences spoken during JFK's ride into the sunset was "We're in nut country now." And that guy had never even heard of Jones, Switzer, and Irvin.

No wonder this town has nowhere else to look for solace but to its football team.

Face it, the Big D stands for Dullsville, a flat featureless plain that has given the United States three things that can remotely be called worthwhile: an airport bigger than most Third World countries; more strip joints per square mile than any city this side of Bangkok; and the Dallas Cowboys. The first two I can live with. The third, I can't.

But it is the only one that Dallas can't live without.

The Dallas Cowboys embody the Bubba-skulled macho culture that says winning not only *is* everything, it absolves everything—be it crime, drug abuse, sexual indiscretion, or just plain ol' arrogance.

It is the kind of culture that celebrates the Michael Irvins and Deion Sanderses of the world for being boors but wonders if Troy Aikman is gay because he thinks a little bit and refrains from pawing at the tits in what are euphemistically known as "gentlemen's clubs."

Not that the Dallas culture is all bad, mind you. It also gave us the Dallas Cowboys Cheerleaders, who are lovely—if not bright. I mean, if they were, wouldn't they have come up with this cheer for Michael Irvin by now: "Oh, Mickey, you so fine. We love the way you blow a line"?

A chant like that could reach all the way to the White House. Or is it the white house, home of snow jobs and blow jobs and "self-employed models" willing to take the rap for their 'Boys?

Can I tell you about Blue Monday in Dallas? They are the days after a Cowboys loss, in which it has been determined by studies that productivity of Dallas workers takes a sharp decline. Can you imagine anything more pathetic than an entire city going into a depression because Emmitt couldn't make fourth-and-one? Maybe only the sound of 70,000 (presumably) full-grown adults shouting "Moose!" in unison.

One-horse town, thy name is Dallas.

Where else would people line up for the autograph of a man about to plead no contest to a felony drug possession? But then, what else could you expect from a city where the man in question, one Michael Irvin, thinks he has a pretty good shot at making the first down simply by asking the cops, "Can I tell you who I am?" Come to think of it, with rap like that, it's amazing they ever brought him in.

But then, this is a city that loves the team that brought in Barry Switzer, a character so brazenly amoral that he makes his predecessor, Jimmy Johnson, seem as upright and trustworthy as Jimmy Carter. Where Landry was a legendary tight-ass, Switzer is as loose as Cream of Wheat.

Forget, for a moment, that in Oklahoma, Switzer ran one of the most outrageous outlaw football programs in the history of college athletics. Disregard his moments of, shall we say, low tolerance, such as when he publicly criticized his quarterback, Troy Aikman, while privately questioning Aikman's sexual preference.

All one needs to know about Barry Switzer is this: He slept with the wife of his best friend and right-hand man at Oklahoma, Larry Lacewell. Now Lacewell works for Switzer as the Cowboys' director of player personnel. Can't say I blame him. After all, what's a marriage worth compared to being one of the 'Boys?

But Switzer is only a symptom of the disease that is Jerry Jones, the Cowboys' owner and the source from which all of the sickness infecting this franchise flows. He is the mother of all meddling owners, a George M. Shitkicker III, if you will, who at least was smart enough to realize that the only way he could ever get the chance to coach an NFL team was to buy one.

He is the one who saw fit to march across the Giants Stadium field during a game practically holding hands with Phil Knight, the Marshall Applewhite of Nike Nation, who thought it was a bargain to pay the Cowboys $2.5 million a year to have the "swoosh" tattooed everywhere in Dallas but on Jerry's ass.

He is the one who bestowed a $13.5 million signing bonus upon Deion Sanders, who has made even fewer tackles than Brian Bosworth.

And he is the one who helps Charles Haley take off his jersey after games like some starstruck clubhouse kid, the one who looked the other way on the decadence of Michael Irvin but couldn't live with the presence of Jimmy Johnson—who had just as much ego and far more hair than Jerry.

Jones is the quintessential rich nerd from hell, and thank heavens he has found the city that deserves him. After all, where else could he find suckers to pay $28 for Texas Stadium parking?

Then there is Emmitt Smith, some sort of freakish, sawed-off tailback god to the Cowboy fans but quite another matter to the reporters who cover him. And the opponents who face him. "Emmy" Smith is what they call him, after the award given to TV hams for acting jobs nowhere near as convincing as the ones Emmitt pulled writhing on the turf. Not content with setting yardage and touchdown records, "Emmy" Smith is now vying for that rare single-season honor of calling for the stretcher more often than for the ball.

But Smith is a Spartan compared with Prime Time Sanders, who doesn't even bother to put on his thigh pads because he knows that any contact he makes on the football field will be purely accidental. If there were any truth in advertising, Deion's nickname would be Sideline Sanders, because that is the first place he heads when things get rough. He would rather take Tim McCarver to dinner than take a route across the middle of the field—and who could blame him? A guy could get hurt in there. If Sanders titled his autobiography *They Call Me Assassin*, he would no doubt be referring to his prowess with an ice bucket.

Speaking of prowess, can someone tell me why Erik Williams videotapes every one of his bedroom, er, adventures? Surely this must be for no one's enjoyment but his own. And even that is suspect. At six-five, 335 pounds, Erik Williams will never be confused with Billy Dee Williams. Presumably, Williams began engaging in the unusual sin-metopgraphy to protect himself from unwarranted charges of sexual assault, like the one he was accused of—and ultimately cleared of—a couple of years back and again last year. My guess is that a stud like Fat Erik either has a closet full of XXX-rated videos or none at all. If I were a betting man, my money would be on the latter.

Which brings us down—yes, *down* is the word—to Michael Irvin, too much of whose money apparently went up his nose, which has very expensive tastes. His apologists in Dallas say this is the inevitable outcome of his childhood, where, as one of seventeen brothers and sisters, he had to grab for everything with both hands and never internalized the concept of self-restraint. As they say in Texas: Cowshit, pardnah. Irvin is the epitome of the pampered athlete who acts the thug simply because he can get away with it.

Who else would choose to spend his thirtieth birthday not with his family but with two "self-employed models" in a drug motel room? What other Sunday-afternoon hero would then try to have one of the women take the rap for him? Who else would show up in court to face felony drug charges dressed like Superfly, with more jewelry around his neck than Cartier's has in its window, and be mobbed by adoring, mostly female, fans (one of whom asked him to sign a Bible)? And where else would such a character be extolled, not excoriated?

Probably in a lot of places where there is nothing else to do but cheer on football players to do the things you wish you could do yourself. But nowhere more vigorously than in the Big D, where the Cowboys are a religion. If so, consider me an atheist, a heretic, the Devil incarnate.

Can I tell you who I am? I think you already know!

MERCURY MORRIS

IF YOU GREW UP, as I did, in Pittsburgh in the 1960s, you followed the Steelers—the Steelers of Bobby Layne, Buddy Dial, John Henry Johnson, and those ugly yellow-and-black uniforms. But they still weren't the ugliest uniforms of that era. That honor belonged to the Dallas Cowboys—or, as I called them then, the Dallas "Clownboys."

Remember those funny white-and-blue jerseys with about fifty stars, like the flag, running up and down their entire shoulder and part of their sleeves? That wasn't the only funny thing about the Cowboys back then. They had this little guy named Eddie LeBaron, a little quarterback I identified with (he being smaller than me at five foot nine), who always seemed to be running for his life against anybody's defense in the NFL.

Those were some of my earliest memories of the Cowboys, back when they basically stunk. However, those memories were hardly my last.

After the Dolphins' 1972 perfect season, Don Shula

EUGENE "MERCURY" MORRIS was a running back for the Miami Dolphins and the San Diego Chargers from 1969 through 1976.

coined the phrase "17–0 Says It All." For the 1960 Cowboys, "0–12 Says It All"—although, to tell the truth, they did tie one game in their inaugural season. Through 1965 they had made some obscure stabs at respectability, but the 'Pokes still hadn't broken the .500 benchmark of mediocrity after six years of existence. And they still weren't as popular around the Dallas area as the Texas–Oklahoma game in the Cotton Bowl.

Why 1965? The year 1965 was also when I first set foot in the state of mind called Texas and found out what the "Whole 'Nother Country" was all about.

Once upon a time in the West . . . I was on my way down to West Texas State to begin what I hoped was to be my college football career. My journey down to West Texas, through Amarillo, began with one of those storied family good-byes at Greater Pittsburgh Airport. Only this good-bye by an eighteen-year-old to my folks wasn't like one today. Back in those days, before air buses, ramps, metal detectors, and all the modern inconveniences of modern-day air travel, it was a simple good-bye at the bottom of a Boeing 707 as you mounted the twenty or thirty steps attached to a truck before you got on the plane. Once you were seated, a stewardess came by handing out minipacks of cigarettes—free Winstons and Salems. They thought they were doing you a favor. Today they arrest you if you even think about smoking aboard a plane. That's how long ago it was.

My plane landed in a little airport in Amarillo, Gate 2 or 3, I'm not sure which. I know it wasn't Gate 1, because there was no Gate 1—I guess they just wanted the airport to seem bigger than it actually was. I guess I should have learned something, right then and there, about Texans' sense of self-appointed significance, which we will refer to as "Texas S.A.S."

There would be yet another indication. As I walked through the gate, I couldn't help but notice a small gift shop at the end of the entryway. And in the window was a comb. Not just an ordinary comb, but a comb about six feet tall and three feet wide. Underneath this mutha of all combs was a sign reading, "Everything is BIG in Texas." To me, that expressed the state's attitude about everything, or "Texas S.A.S."

I had a pretty good career at West Texas State. No, make that an outstanding career. In my junior year I finished second in the country in rushing to that USC boy O. J. Simpson. And by the way, Juice *never* led the nation during the season—for nine-tenths of the year I led— but somehow, someway, he nosed me out in the last game, and we all know about the horseshoe he has up his butt!

And if that wasn't bad enough, I had as a teammate someone named Duane Thomas. And he was one helluva player. But more about Duane later.

So what happens? Having had such a great junior year, I got letters of inquiry from the Cowboys expressing interest in me. And here—and now let me slip into a Texas drawl—I said, "Hot dang! I'm gonna be a Cowboy!" At that point, I actually liked the Cowboys. Especially when I had visions of playing in Dallas.

But—and there's always a *but*—by my senior year, the Cowboys had become more interested in Duane than in yours truly. Maybe it was because they had watched his progress at West Texas. Or maybe it was because of his size—after all, he was six foot two, 205 pounds, and I was only five foot ten, 185 pounds. Or maybe, just maybe, it was because he was a native of Texas, a "Dallas Boy"—their phrase, not mine.

Whatever. Despite the fact that I had led the nation in

rushing all of my senior year and set all kinds of rushing records and broken those I hadn't set, the Cowboys looked to Calvin Hill, Grant's dad, as their first draft pick in 1969. The next year, of course, they picked Duane as their number-one draft choice. That sorta pissed me off!

And even though Duane became Rookie of the Year in 1970 and a full-fledged star in the NFL, he was something less of a star down in the Lone Star State, and its state of mind, when, for some reason, he began demeaning the sainted Tom Landry. Duane called Landry a "plastic man" and said that Landry was "programmed." You know . . . black militant talk. And naturally, a black man in the 1970s wasn't supposed to say those kinds of things in public about a respected white man in Dallas. Especially a God-fearing Christian like Landry. And so Duane immediately became an expendable commodity, both to that great legion of Billy Joe Bobs who were the heart and soul of the Dallas supporters and to the Dallas team itself. And they ultimately traded his ass to the Chargers.

Through the years you can see why people never liked the Dallas Cowboys persona. But I personally didn't like them because of what they did to the Dolphins in Super Bowl VI. It wasn't just that they beat us, 24–3; it was how they beat the shit out of us, then rubbed our noses in it. Maybe we had forgotten that they, the Cowboys, had had their asses kicked in Super Bowl V by the Colts (hey!), or maybe they hadn't. But it didn't matter, because they did us all a favor by beating us.

I mean, the Dolphins had all treated the game like we were Cinderella, just happy to be at the Big Dance. We had also forgotten how to play the game of football that Sunday in New Orleans.

After the game I made a comment to the press that if

I had played more—and I had played (returning four kickoffs for 90 yards), but if I had played *more*—we would have won! Later, in the locker room, I had a confrontation with coach Don Shula. I told him that if he gave me a chance to play in the 1972 season, I'd provide what was missing in the Dolphins' attack.

The next year, if you'll remember, we went 17–0, and I won a starting job, rushed for 1,000 yards (on the button), and scored twelve times, to lead the league. But everyone on the team—Bob Griese, Larry Csonka, Jim Kiick, Jim Mandich, Larry Little, Nick Buoniconti, Dick Anderson, Earl Morrall, everybody—did more because of the ass-whuppin' the Cowboys gave us in Super Bowl VI. And we had determined, even before the season started, never ever to let it happen again.

Now that we have established that the Dolphins had set the all-time record of 17–0, the "perfect season," let me get back to the subject at hand: the Dallas Cowboys. Today they're somewhat unpopular and people cheer for them to get beat. They used to have players like Eddie LeBaron, Don Meredith, Roger Staubach, and even Danny "No, Danny, No" White—heroes all. Today they have a group with a totally different personality.

My grandmother used to say to me, "You know, Eugene, you're really smart, but in a way nobody likes." And when I think of the Dallas Cowboys, I think of them in the same way—they're really good, *but* in a way nobody likes. They have an attitude that engenders a dislike for them. Example? Troy Aikman with his "no-smile" approach typifies what the Cowboys stand for, and that's all business. The other part of the team, and equation, is a caricature of rampant self-indulgence and self-glorification. When you look at this group, a group declaring itself to be what some call "America's Team," you can't help but somewhat dislike them. And root for them to lose.

As for me, I want them to get beat the way they beat us back in that 1972 Super Bowl. It still sticks in my craw, sort of sour grapes, if you will. Oh, we did get even with them two seasons later, in 1973, in the first Thanksgiving Day game the Cowboys ever lost. We beat the shit out of them down there in front of their fans. They needed that game, tied as they were with the Redskins, and we didn't. And we kicked their asses in their own living room, in Texas Stadium. That was a measure of satisfaction—one, like the ad says, that "keeps on giving."

But over and above my personal satisfaction for having gotten even, the Cowboys were always the kind of team you never wanted to see win—whether against you or against anyone else, for that matter. Especially now. Why? Because the Dolphins of the early 1970s were one of football's special teams, and I don't ever want to hear some Dallas flannelmouth compare the Cowboys of today—or any day—to the "perfect" Dolphins of that era.

Also, and I have to say this, I don't feel bad because they have all that in-house stuff going on right now—all those outside distractions, you might call them. The irony is that the clowns in those silly uniforms back in the early days of their franchise are really the same guys today, but in different uniforms. Only today they're no longer funny. Remember when being drunk used to be funny? Remember Foster Brooks? You don't see him around anymore, do you? Same with the Cowboys; they're no longer funny, warm, or fuzzy.

Now, I'm not saying everyone should dislike the Cowboys. Keep in mind that the Cowboys were the first to bring out Las Vegas show girls on the sidelines and change the visual landscape of sports. They were the first to have real cleavage on cheerleaders—*very* grown up. In fact, they are the closest thing around to *Playboy* Playmates. When I was playing, we had little cheerleaders that were maybe twelve or thirteen years old. But Dallas changed all that. . . .

However, the Dallas Cowboy Cheerleaders are only the start or, as they say, the tip of the iceberg. Today, as individuals *and* as a team, they have created a gangsta image. Using "Archie Bunker logic," they've got too many "soul brothers" on the team now, too many black "dudes" influencing too many things going on outside the realm of just plain ol' football. Or so the "white man's reasoning" goes. But no matter whose logic it is, it seems that for the Cowboys, it's business as usual—cockiness on the field, scandals up the ying-yang off the field.

To what can we trace this lack of good old-fashioned discipline, the discipline instilled in the 'Boys by Tom Landry? The lack of respect, morality, or manners? There's an old sports saying: Whatever you've got in the front office, that's what you have on the field. Whatever it is, it must come from the top or from the head coach. From a Tom Landry, whom you could respect, you went to a Jimmy Johnson, who always seemed to be as interested in how good his hair looked as in how good his team looked. And now you have Barry Switzer, who, oddly enough, reminds me of Don Shula in his last years. Don couldn't control the new kind of player drawn from the new kind of "gene pool" in our society; and Barry inherited a cast of Wild West characters.

To understand the Cowboys and their mentality, you must understand their roots—and I mean that in both a literal and figurative sense: from a scrappy, expansion,

down-at-the-bottom-of-the-heap team to an intimidating,
we-can-beat-anybody-anytime powerhouse. It's a very
interesting line of progression, almost like that of our
society, which has changed in the thirty-seven years the
Cowboys have been around. Like today, it's an in-your-
face attitude.

By the time both football and society had entered the
1980s, we had entered an era of "looking good and looking out for number-one"—the Me Decade, they called it.
And by the end of the 1980s, Tom Landry had lost control of his players, all playing the "Me" Formation. By
the end of the 1988 season, I remember seeing Landry
down on the field in that stingy-brim hat, the kind my
dad used to wear back in the 1960s, for the last time in
his twenty-nine-year coaching career, the last time he
was on the sidelines as the only coach the Cowboys ever
had. His team, 3–13, was almost back to where his first
edition had started, back in those funny-looking uniforms twenty-nine years before. It was a sad ending to a
grand and glorious career. But it was understandable.
As an old-time coach, he had become out of touch with
the modern-day athlete, the kind of athlete who thinks
of himself first and his team second—if he ever thinks
of his team at all. Today that's called *no* loyalty. But
loyalty is not a relevant consideration in sports today.
"Show me the money" has replaced loyalty to one's
team. Today it's "in" to be loyal to the cash game and
live in the fast lane.

And then there was the changing of the guard. Not just
on the sidelines, but in the front office as well. Here was
Jerry Jones in the owner's box, and all of a sudden, his
former college classmate, Jimmy Johnson, was the head
coach. Jimmy Johnson, whose always styled, perfect
hair took the place of Landry's signature hat.

Johnson was the exact opposite of Landry. Whereas Landry's coaching had produced a relentless style of play, and his teams had featured a star-studded cast of clean-cut white guys—guys like Bob Lilly, Don Meredith, Roger Staubach, Chuck Howley, Cliff Harris, Randy White, and players who never drew too much attention to themselves as they kicked everybody's ass who got in their way—Johnson transformed the Cowboys into a team filled with personalities and showboats. It was a generational shift, a social metamorphosis. The new Cowboys saw themselves as entertainers and had a need to draw attention to themselves after what they saw as a good play or a good hit or—even better—a score. Johnson was right at home with this new phenomenon, one of unofficial showboating. Or, as the NFL calls it, "unsportsmanlike showboating," having made the end zone a forbidden planet where you must keep your helmet on and stay away from the camera. Whatever it's called, it's still just another method of taunting as practiced by the Cowboys.

So while Jimmy Johnson had turned the Cowboys into a Super Bowl–winning team, it was still a case of the six-foot comb in the Amarillo airport syndrome, the same mind-set: Everything is bigger in Texas, even the Wild West behavior.

However, some things just got *too* big in Dallas, if that's possible. Like egos. And when Jimmy Johnson's "Hale-Bopp" collided with UFO Jerry Jones, Jimmy had to go, garment bag and all slung over shoulder. His "container" was replaced by Barry Switzer, a handpicked Jones "homeboy." It was just like when we were in school and all of a sudden one day we had a substitute teacher in gym class. Remember, your agenda suddenly became more important than his? Well, Barry was kind of like the substitute gym teacher. Actually, a substitute gym teacher who had an "in" with the principal—which is how he got the job. And, all of a sudden, with the new head coach just glad to be there, the inmates were running the asylum.

And while Johnson had come from a successful program at the University of Miami, Switzer had come from a program at the University of Oklahoma that had been devastated by a series of scandals, of college-age thugs with scholarships, a gene pool known as "student-athletes" from Generation X. Switzer took that mind-set to the Cowboys, and they became a Wild West show, with every player riding off in whatever direction his ego took him. It was a Wild West show such as sports had never seen before, and a fitting metaphor for a team called the Cowboys.

Look at the Cowboys today and you'll get some idea of how much they've changed since the days, and the discipline, of Tom Landry. Now you have the likes of Deion Sanders, Michael Irvin, Leon Lett, Erik Williams, Charles Haley, Emmitt Smith, and many, many others. Switzer looks more like that gym teacher, always looking behind him for the next spitball—or, more correctly, next scandal—than a head coach in charge of his players. And his stars seem more like that Oklahoma team he once coached, one that produced more potential prison inmates than potential NFL players.

All of this to the delight of those who find pleasure in witnessing the Cowboys' problems. But wait! I *do* feel for them. (No, I'm lying!) The 'Pokes are like the West Coast rappers. They have an attitude that the East Coast rappers just don't like. And I don't need a reason to dislike them; that's just the way it is.

Let me tell you something that happened during the

past two seasons, not during those long-ago days when I played for the Dolphins. In Super Bowl XXX, when the Cowboys played the Steelers, I made a bet with a Dolphin rookie who took the Cowboys and gave the points, a "lock," he said. How dare a Dolphin bet on the Cowboys! Sickening! "What is *wrong* with you?" I asked. "Where's your AFC loyalty?" By the way, I covered and won my bet against the Cowboys. I was happy because in my mind, and in my wallet, I had won.

Now, the next Super Bowl, this past one (Super Bowl XXXI, if you're keeping score), the real "America's Team," the Green Bay Packers, beat the New England Patriots in a game that turned out, in betting parlance, to be a "push"—meaning no one won their bets because the winning margin and the point spread were the same. It just goes to show that when the Cowboys aren't around, nobody gets hurt, either in the wallet or in the ego. And everybody walks away happy. Everybody, that is, except the Dallas Cowboys. And ain't that cool? (Smile!)

JIM MURRAY

I DON'T HATE THE Dallas Cowboys. Far from it. Now that we do not have a franchise of our own in L.A., they could very easily be our team.

But when I speak of the Dallas Cowboys, I don't refer to the present class of hoodlums, scofflaws, and anti-heroes wearing the Lone Star helmet. I refer to the America's Team Dallas Cowboys. The John Wayne bunch. The ones that were going to come riding in to save the fort, win the West, hang the rustlers, and defend the Alamo. *Those* Cowboys. Riding off into the sunset with the schoolmarm.

Those were Tom Landry's Cowboys, not Barry Switzer's. They had Roger Staubach, not Michael Irvin. Calvin Hill, not Erik Williams. The coach could be found in church, not in a bar.

The present-day Cowboys' reputation is so salty, they make Deion Sanders look like an altar boy. After all, the worst thing Prime Time does is go on talk shows and say outrageous things. This modern bunch seems to do all their talking to assistant district attorneys.

JIM MURRAY has been a sports columnist for the Los Angeles Times *for thirty-six years and is one of only four sports columnists to win the Pulitzer Prize.*

The team got so closely associated with illicit drug use in the tabloid press (to say nothing of the police blotters) that the wags couldn't resist. America's Team became "South America's Team" or the "Medellín Cartel's Team."

The team used to be owned by this group of shadowy millionaires, the Texas Big Rich who hardly ever appeared on *Hard Copy*. The team was a hobby, not an avocation. They kept a low profile, their pictures were in the papers so seldom only close friends knew what they looked like. Their oil wells were more important to them than their football players.

Now the Cowboys are owned by an Arkansas high roller who gets his picture in the paper as often as his quarterback and is on the field so much, some people think he's a backup center. Jerry Jones comes off as more of a playboy than a tycoon. He's more than a hands-on owner, he's an in-the-huddle owner.

He keeps getting coaches in his own image. Just win, baby! Let someone else worry about the morality involved.

The sport of football used to flourish in this country when the teams suited up real students, when they got their lineups out of the labs, not night court. Coaches were members of the faculty—after all, Knute Rockne taught chemistry his first few years.

Then coaches began to learn that the roughest, toughest elements of the population were not found in student bodies; they were found in street gangs.

There was a problem getting them through academic entrance requirements. But a coach who put in an offensive scheme a George Halas couldn't stop found the challenge a piece of pie. The professors were overmatched.

The public didn't care. They wanted to go to the Rose Bowl, the Super Bowl. They didn't care how they got there. So long as they could paint their faces red and gold and shout, "We're number-one!" Their goal in life was to "Beat State!"

So, that's kind of how the Dallas Cowboys went from America's Team to *America's Most Wanted*. They were just following the rest of the game. Frank Merriwell would be a third-stringer today. If he even made the squad. He might just be picking up towels in the locker room.

The Cowboys became America's Team because Tex Schramm, their general manager in their glory days, dubbed them that.

But Tex was following in the footsteps of an NFL film crew who put together a highlight film in 1979, and the words crept in there.

Tex knew a good thing when he heard it, and the next thing we knew, we all had a team.

The American public has been conditioned since the days of "Broncho Billy" Anderson and the silent film screenings to regard anything in a ten-gallon hat on a horse as an authentic American hero. The Cowboys were a soft sell. Their coach, the laconic, self-reliant Tom Landry, came off as a combination of Clint Eastwood and John Wayne, their players a posse of good guys with the sheriff's star on their helmets.

It was surefire box office. When the Cowboys came to town, the home team sold twice as many tickets. Cowboy gear sold 27 percent of all NFL Properties souvenirs. No one else sold more than 10 percent.

The media picked up on it. "America's Team" had a nice patriotic ring to it. The Cowboys had a nice rollicking cast of characters. Walt Garrison was a real cowboy,

Calvin Hill was a Cowboy from Yale, Dandy Don Meredith was early prime time, a dashing high plains roller. When Roger Staubach won the car for being Super Bowl MVP, he asked them if he could make it a station wagon.

You can see where cocaine and accusations of rape and sexual harassment and female-bashing wouldn't fit this image. Let's face it: Jerry Jones ain't Clint Murchison; Barry Switzer is no Tom Landry; Troy Aikman *could* be another Roger Staubach, but not if he's surrounded by rogues and the lineup got so raunchy, Troy stopped speaking to his coach till he enforced some discipline. And discipline is not Barry Switzer's long suit.

So America hasn't got a team. What we've got is an adult western. The 'Pokes are the guys in the black hats. How in the world did that happen? Whatever would John Wayne, Harry Carey, Gary Cooper, Hoot Gibson, and William S. Hart think? C. B. DeMille would never shoot it. We can always make a documentary: *How the West Was Lost.*

ANDY RUSSELL

DON'T WE ALL WONDER sometimes who, in his or her wild-est imagination, first said that the Dallas Cowboys were America's Team? At least they didn't dub them our Dream Team. America's Team?

Who first burdened the Cowboys with this absurd moniker? Was it some Madison Avenue hotshot who had been asked (presumably by Cowboy management) to come up with a cute slogan to capture our collective imagination? Or was it some serious football fan sitting in North Dakota or Montana who had grown tired of Green Bay's dominance? Maybe it was some TV commentator seeking to add another unneeded superlative to his rhetoric. One pal of mine thought it might be because they were the first team to have cheerleaders, who just happened to be gorgeous.

We know that there are a certain number of people who always prefer the underdog, which, of course, was exactly the role played so convincingly by Dallas when they took on the in-Vince-able (Lombardi). Weren't we all a little tired of the Packers winning every year? Yes,

---

ANDY RUSSELL was a linebacker for the Pittsburgh Steelers in 1963 and from 1966 through 1976.

Bart Starr, Ray Nitschke, and the boys were hugely impressive, but one did long for a new team to stop the Pack's unrelenting march to the NFL title every year. For a while Dallas was our only hope. But America's Team? I don't think so!

First of all, Dallas is in Texas, not a state universally loved by those of us who live elsewhere. Many of us, I suspect, think of Texans in general (and I know it's always wrong to generalize—but don't we all do it?) as rather rough, sometimes crude, occasionally vulgar, prone to bragging (about living in the biggest state), swaggering, cowboy-boot-wearing, overly loud, obnoxious folks. The men, mostly potbellied, wear little thin strings for ties, and their high-maintenance women all seem to dye their hair and wear too much makeup and heavy gold jewelry. Isn't Dallas the home of face-lifts and tummy tucks? Am I being too harsh here? Hey, I'm sure there are some real nice folks living in Dallas, but we're talking about its overall image here. How could this city ever produce the *real* America's Team?

Second, Dallas is certainly not to be confused with one of our great landmark cities, like New York, Chicago, Boston, or San Francisco. Dallas is known for what? The home office of insurance companies, real-estate developers (who sucked a number of S&Ls dry by building enough office space for the year 2020—but in the 1980s), and oil and gas producers, whose ability to tout a questionable location (dry holes beware) are not exactly something to admire.

Where is culture, character, values, and substance when one thinks of Dallas, where a man's reputation is too often judged simply by the size of his wallet (or house or plane or boat—yes, there are actually some lakes in Dallas), the number of acres or cows he owns, or how many BMWs or Mercedes he drives? When we think of Dallas, we think of overspending, extravagance, arrogance, and yet an insecurity—yes, a fear of never living up to its flashy PR, knowing it can't back up its contrived image. Unfortunately, don't we all think of J.R. Ewing of the *Dallas* TV show when we think of the Big D?

Dallas just will never be America's anything, except, perhaps, the king of overhype, self-indulgence, and over-reaching. Well, enough of this Dallas-bashing. Perhaps I did get somewhat carried away. I certainly don't want to push those of you who have always naturally disliked Dallas into feeling sorry for it or its flashy populace.

If not Dallas, what team might rightly be called America's Team? It would have to be a team that represents traits that Americans value—hard work, discipline, poise, class, toughness, strength, and straightforward-ness. Is there a team that epitomizes all these traits? Well, here is one slightly biased, prone-to-overreaching, certainly prejudiced person's damn-the-counter-arguments theory. I believe the real America's Team has existed for years in a city that no one would expect but finally came to be given its due: the Pittsburgh Steelers.

What? you say. How could this be? You think Pittsburgh is one of America's ugliest cities, covered with soot from all the steel mills, bathed in coal dust, where rivers catch fire. Not hardly, folks. Pittsburgh is definitely America's best-kept secret. If you saw the recent Rand McNally national survey showing Pittsburgh as America's most livable city, you probably scoffed at the rating, believing that the survey was somehow bogus.

But it's true. It's really a great place. I was drafted (by the Steelers) to this city, after having lived in Detroit,

Chicago, New York, and St. Louis, and quickly understood that Pittsburgh is a very special place. Since I'm not a native, I feel free to brag about Pittsburgh. Perhaps you think I have no perspective. Hey, like many people, I've been lucky enough to see a lot of this world—I've seen Sydney Harbor, viewed Hong Kong from Victoria Peak, enjoyed a few beers at the Hoffbrauhaus in Munich, walked across the wooden bridge in Lucerne, sipped champagne overlooking the Eiffel Tower, been sleepless in Seattle, and enjoyed San Fran. I've also seen the little gems like Siena, Rothenburg, Baden-Baden, Bruges, Cape Town, and Telluride. Please note that none of the special places listed above have a football team. Believe me, Pittsburgh is one terrific city.

Thanks to the progressive thinking of such industrial giants as Mellon, Carnegie, Heinz, Westinghouse, and Hillman, Pittsburgh's skies no longer rain coal dust, the rivers flow clear with game fish, and the skyline is tall and true. This is an old, American city full of tradition and ethnic heritage. It is a beautiful city that has never gotten its credit, and incidentally, it had, and has, one hell of a football team.

Who does real America respect more—Dandy Don Meredith or Terry Bradshaw? Michael Irvin or Lynn Swann? Hollywood Henderson or Jack Lambert? Too Tall Jones or Joe Greene? Duane Thomas or Franco Harris? Is there any question? (Granted, I've ignored some truly high-caliber Cowboys: Roger Staubach, Lee Roy Jordan, Pete Gent, Jethro Pugh, Chuck Howley, Cliff Harris, and Bob Lilly—but hey, hello, I'm trying to make a point here.)

Clearly the Steelers have been the better team, having won two of three Super Bowl confrontations. But there is obviously more to the America's Team title than just athletic excellence. There is what a team stands for, its basic character, its style, its substance.

The Pittsburgh teams have always represented the blue-collar worker, from the steel mills, the foundries, and other heavy industry located up and down the three rivers (the Monongahela and the Allegheny, which define the borders of the city proper and form the Ohio). Pittsburgh is a tough town, where hard men and even tougher women put in a good day's work before stopping on the way home for an "Imp and Iron" (a shot of Imperial whiskey and an Iron City beer). Who would the majority of real America (not Madison Avenue's pick) respect more—an open-hearth furnace operator or an insurance clerk; a coal miner or a fast-food operator; a construction worker or a real-estate developer?

To me, Dallas the city always seemed like it tried too hard to be sophisticated and slick, and eventually the team, despite Tom Landry's strong moral fiber, started to look and act like the city.

Chuck Noll told us before the 1975 Super Bowl in Miami against Dallas that "the Cowboys will to try to fool us. They're going to show us all those multiple sets, with all kinds of motion, and hope we make a mistake. They want to trick, confuse, and outfinesse us. They are not going to line up, like we are, and run the ball right down their throat. This is a team that relies on deception. We will defeat this team."

Most American men (and some women whose fathers helped them appreciate the game) grew up believing that yards and then touchdowns had to be earned the hard way, with hard-nosed blocking and tackling, not with gimmicks, finesse plays, and tricks.

Granted, not many Americans were even aware of the Pittsburgh Steelers in the early years, despite teams full of wonderful characters such as Ernie Stautner, Bobby Layne, Big Daddy Lipscomb, Tom "the Bomb" Tracey, Joe Krupa, Myron Pottios, John Henry Johnson, Red Mack, and Frank Atkinson. These were hard men who believed in hard work and hard play afterward. Hey, even Johnny Unitas, Len Dawson, and Jack Kemp went through Pittsburgh before finding themselves elsewhere. Many of the less famous Steelers were playing football just to avoid working in the mines or the mills.

These players were legends (granted, for some, only in their own minds) and brought the younger players a sense of history, a commitment to excellence and courage. I will never forget when, during my rookie year, Ernie Stautner, the (now) Hall of Fame defensive tackle, came into our huddle with a compound fracture of the thumb. Without saying anything, he wrenched the broken thumb back into his palm and continued to play. Later, on the sidelines, he asked for tape and bandaged it himself. After the game, showing his injury to the team doctor, Stautner said, "Hey, Doc, I might have a problem here!" The doctor then took off the tape and attended to all that blood and bare bone.

Stautner taught us young players that playing hurt was a badge of honor. This was old-fashioned, ass-kicking, brutal football the way it was meant to be played, before the rule makers made it "safer." He also taught us no less impressive lessons, like how to drink shots and beer and always still be a gentleman—no matter how grungy a bar it was.

The Cowboys franchise didn't start until 1960, and those players had no one to teach them, no one to leave them a legacy of honor—you play the game not for money but for pride. We were blessed to have Mr. Arthur Rooney, the "Chief," who won (or was it lost?) one of the oldest franchises in the league in a poker game, walking through our locker room after every game, win or lose, patting us on the back, asking us if we were okay and telling us we had done a good job, wishing us "a lotta luck" the next game. For the Chief, it wasn't all about money, and he wasn't looking for publicity. Promotional gimmicks like cheerleaders, fancy baseball caps, and Nike swooshes were not part of the Pittsburgh Steelers—this was rough-and-tough football, played in the trenches, and it wasn't supposed to be glamorous. The Chief didn't care about getting his name in the sports pages, and as an ex-boxer, he only wanted his "boys" to play tough ball, give it all they had and come out of it healthy. Mr. Rooney was genuine in his concern, and it made us want to perform well for him, not just for ourselves.

There are too many stories to tell about those old Steeler greats and the quality organization that went untold by the national media. America didn't wake up to the Pittsburgh Steelers until the great teams of the Seventies, when the Steelers won four of six Super Bowls.

In fact, no team could really have been considered America's Team before the decade of the seventies because that was when television really began selling the game, making it America's new pastime, replacing baseball. During this time, NFL Films, Inc., produced those almost magical NFL highlight films, elevating the game to some sort of martial arts ballet, showing it to be the drama it really was. There was Pete Rozelle, the genius promoter and commissioner, putting together NFL Properties, selling every kid in the country his favorite player's jersey. The NFL didn't come into its own until the 1970s.

The Pittsburgh Steelers, the team that dominated that

decade, became a team this country could grow to love. And it did. There was Terry Bradshaw being carried off the field on a stretcher at halftime and then returning to throw the winning touchdown pass in the fourth quarter—Terry's sense of theater was always superb. There was Franco Harris making his "Immaculate Reception" to beat the Raiders on the last play of the playoff game in 1972. There was Joe Greene, surely the player of the decade, smothering runners and sacking the opponent's quarterbacks. There was Jack Lambert, the guy others claimed was so mean that he didn't even like himself, chewing nails and intimidating opponents. And then there was Lynn Swann, the former ballet student, and John Stallworth, who set new standards for NFL body control, soaring, and then hanging in midair, to make acrobatic catches, the likes of which had never before been seen in the NFL—even Nureyev would have been astonished at some of those amazing catches.

That team was full of heroes America could relate to. There was Rocky Bleier, a war hero, wounded in Vietnam, miraculously gaining 1,000 yards on his wounded legs. There was Jack Ham, perhaps the finest linebacker ever to play the game, dropping runners in their tracks behind the line of scrimmage and intercepting Kenny Stabler on the final play of the game to ensure the Steelers' first Super Bowl appearance.

There were many unsung heroes who played hurt in the trenches (players like Ray Mansfield, who played with a broken neck; Dwight White, who came out of the hospital with a terrible flu to play superbly in the first Super Bowl win against Minnesota; and Moon Mullins ignoring his concussions. None of these players asked for any credit; they just got the job done, the way real Americans would respect).

You say the team was too predictable, too boring—not enough colorful characters to really set the team apart from the NFL's athletic norm? What about "Fats" Holmes, who cut his hair into the shape of an arrowhead, to point the direction he was going to take, into the opponent's backfield? How about L. C. Greenwood, known as "Hollywood Bags," who wore gold high-top shoes to accentuate his blinding speed upfield? What about Frenchy Fuqua, known as the "Count," who wore high-heeled glass shoes with goldfish in the heels? The Count and Hollywood had an annual dress-off in the locker room to vie for the title of Best Dressed (or most absurdly dressed) Steeler. There was Mel Blount, with his shaved head (way before Michael Jordan), making opponents' wide receivers seemingly disappear. No, the Steelers were not boring. They played hard, partied hard, and had plenty of color.

There are just too many Steelers to mention, let alone describe in detail, but this country revered them. Seven of them (from the 1970s) are already in the Hall of Fame (Greene, Bradshaw, Harris, Ham, Lambert, Blount, and the coach, Chuck Noll). Coach Noll taught great players to play with maximum intensity, concentration, discipline, class, and dignity. I believe this country grew to respect that team, to adopt that team as theirs, and to ultimately, yes, even love that team.

You say, What about today's teams? You are not interested in history, just what's happening now. You don't live in the past, right? Well, have you watched the Cowboys of the Nineties swagger around the field, strut their stuff, do their trash-talking, give their sumo impressions, flaunt their successes in their opponents' faces, and goose-step their way around the end zone? Have you heard them brag about their accomplishments, ridicule their opponents, and seemingly ignore their coach? Do you really feel that these are the values that most Americans respect?

Granted, today's Cowboys are a very talented bunch. But, for my taste, too few of them behave properly. They are not exactly a group that one would confuse with what this country admires, a group whose work ethic and on-the-field behavior (we won't even mention off-the-field) leaves much to be admired. When one thinks of words like *humility, character, class,* and *dignity,* does one ever think of the Dallas Cowboys? Fathers and mothers certainly don't want them as role models for their children. Wives don't want their sons and husbands confusing this behavior with what is acceptable, not to mention admirable.

The Cowboys as America's Team . . . please!

The current Steelers, whose tenacious defense, with stars like defensive backs Rod Woodson (certainly a better all-around player than Deion Sanders), Carnell Lake, and linebacker Greg Lloyd, bottled up the Cowboys' offense in the 1996 Super Bowl, shutting down their powerful running game in the second half when it counted, coming within an eyelash of upsetting the Cowboys.

If it weren't for a couple of gift touchdowns presented on a platter by Steeler quarterback Neil O'Donnell, they might have won. Neil, who had had a great year (the team wouldn't have gotten to the Super Bowl without him), was clearly forcing some passes that even Neil would now agree shouldn't have been thrown. He was trying too hard, a trait America, even in defeat, would find difficult to criticize. His coach, Bill Cowher, with his Kirk Douglas chin jutting out to show his toughness and commitment, stood up for his failed quarterback, taking responsibility for the loss that was so close to being a win—Cowher just had too much class to make excuses. He is a true Steeler.

The Cowboys did not earn the victory but won despite themselves. I attended the game and was astounded at the sea of black and gold (Steeler colors) throughout the stadium. When Dallas moved the ball early in the game, jumping out to a ten-point lead, there was very little noise and excitement shown by the spectators. But in the second half, the place was really rocking as the Steelers made their comeback. This was clearly an overwhelmingly pro-Steeler crowd, even though statistics show that people from all over the country attend the Super Bowl—not just folks from the Burgh and the Big D.

Larry Brown, the Dallas cornerback who made those interceptions, was totally out of position, beaten badly, but still, somewhat absurdly, named the MVP of the game. When asked about those interceptions, a former Cowboy defensive back told me, "If O'Donnell hadn't thrown those balls totally off the mark, Brown should have been cut from the team." Interestingly, both O'Donnell and Brown have now moved on to other teams.

What is my point? It is that the current Steelers, a huge underdog, outweighed on the line by more than fifty pounds per man without the highly paid superstars, played the Cowboys to within an inch of their football lives. Yes, Dallas won, but there was no strutting, no high-stepping—the Cowboys knew they had barely escaped with their win.

Dallas was Goliath, Pittsburgh was David. But this time Goliath won because David's stones whizzed by the big guy's shoulders. Do you really think, America, that we choose Goliath as our favorite competitor?

BUDD SCHULBERG

THE PSYCHOLOGY OF CHOOSING your favorite team in
SportsWorld, and your particular *unfavorite*, is a complex problem. And it's fascinated me all my life. Why was
I, for instance—a sports nut from California grammar
school days onward—a natural Dodger fan even in the
pre–Jackie Robinson days? What was there about the
Bums in Brooklyn's Ebbetts Field that got to me when I
was still going to L.A. High? Why did I take it so personally when Mickey Owen dropped that fateful third strike
in our desperate World Series game with the New York
Yankees?

You see, we driven spectator-sportsmen are irration-
ally possessive about "our" team. For some inexplicable
reason buried in our cultural pattern or our DNA, it's *us*
against *them*.

So just as I became a Dodger fan (and stayed one till
my team betrayed its roots and set up shop in tonier
L.A., leaving me to root for the lowly Mets), I became

BUDD SCHULBERG is the author of What Makes Sammy
Run?, The Disenchanted, *and* The Harder They Fall, *and
screenwriter of the Academy Award–winning film* On the
Waterfront.

devotedly anti-Yankee. Yes, I know, there's Babe and Lou, and Mickey and Joe, and Whitey and Yogi, and a gaggle of lovable Yanks—how can you put the Yanks on your enemy list? Well, one very good reason was that they were too good. Too many pennants, world championships—it seemed every year. And something else— even with lowlifes like Billy Martin—too clean, too respectable, the sweet smell of Establishment about them.

Still, I could love the Dodgers without quite getting myself to hate the Yankees. I admired the Yankees. I respected the Yankees. And I definitely did not like the Yankees. And I still don't. Not even the glorious '96ers. They were still George Steinbrenner's team, and in this corner, rooting for Steinbrenner was only a shade less reprehensible than rooting for Kaltenbrunner in World War II.

But *hate* is a strong word, a verbal nasty; are we not taught in our generous Judeo-Christian tradition to love our enemies? From our Old Testament prophets to Jesus to Martin Luther King, Jr., we are urged to love them. But how, fellow football fanatics, can you love the Cowboys? I mean, unless you come from Dallas or are kissin' cousins of Jerry Jones or suffer from some other sports-spectator disorder, are you not more apt to say, "Love thine enemy, my ass! No way I'm gonna love the Dallas Cowboys"? In fact, for reasons unquestionably irrational but also deeply felt, I hate the Dallas Cowboys. There, I've said it. I'm feeling a little better already. If confession is good for the soul, so is a healthy hatred like this one for the 'Boys.

And I'm not a Jerry-come-lately hater, either. But it does start with Jerry Jones, the Arkansas hustler with the Texas-sized ego, and his merry men, led by superstar Michael Irvin, who comes to his drug trial sporting

a full-length mink coat, designer shades, diamond earrings, gold chains, tailored threads—in lavender yet—
alligator shoes, and a sense of values that included his
warning a friend of the topless dancers busted with Irvin
that she'd better not cooperate with the D.A. because
he of the gifted hands and the global ego was so much
"more powerful," that if you double-cross me, "you'll
never see . . . the light of day again, I promise you . . ."
Or so she told the court.

A role model? Definitely, especially if you aspire to
membership in the Gambino or Luchese family. Nor is
Modest Michael the Lone Ranger of the Bad 'Boys.
There's plenty of frisky company on the Jerry Jones–
Barry Switzer Express, including celebrated suspendees
Erik Williams and Leon Lett. Asked about a notorious
party house for fun-loving Cowboys, nice and close to
the team's H.Q., their teammate on the offensive line,
Nate Newton, reflected the team's lofty moral tone,
"Outside of murder, you can't do too much wrong on
our team."

The only murders they were committing in the 1990s
were against the opposition, winning three out of four
Super Bowls, and doing it not with the class and competitive grace of the San Francisco 49ers, but with arrogance and bully-boy braggadocio that made hating the
Cowboys a highly enjoyable and absolutely irresistible
experience.

But I've had an awful lot of practice. You're talking to
a Cowboy-hater who's put in some thirty years of good,
healthy, time-consuming animosity. Let's flash back
those thirty years to the reign of Tom Landry. I didn't
like his grim, thin lips. I didn't like the haughtiness, the
coldness, the sanctimonious stare. I didn't like his hat. I
didn't like the way people were beginning to call him

God's coach. With Mr. Perfect, Roger Staubach, standing tall in God's pocket, they began this annoying habit of winning games, winning conference titles, and winning Super Bowls that's made us miserable, with only a few happy lapses (and losses) in between.

As if the "God's coach" bit wasn't enough, they somehow became "America's Team," which was for us Giant fans—and Redskin and Packer, Steeler, Dolphin, and 49er fans—akin to naming John Gotti "America's Number One Boy Scout." A superabundance of hubris, that's what raised the hackles of us Cowboy-abominators. And all the time Tom Landry was pacing those sidelines, so piously and righteously, a bunch of his boys from the Sixties to the Eighties were just as outrageous, out-of-hand, and above the law as the latter-day Jones (and Jimmy Johnson) boys. Have we forgotten Landry's flamboyant linebacker "Hollywood" Henderson, who snorted cocaine during Super Bowl XIII and now scratches out a living making motivational speeches confessing to his sins? And All-Pro end Harvey Martin, who's also owned up to using drugs while playing for the Landry 'Boys. Defensive end Larry Bethea made a lot of big plays on the field but lost his life to drugs. And Michael Irvin and Co. didn't exactly invent sex scandals for the Cowboys. Wide receiver Lance Rentzel and kicker Rafael Septien were caught out of bounds in the Landry era in separate incidents with ten-year-old girls. And legendary are the tales of Too Tall Jones's way of celebrating Memorial Day, in patriotic tribute to America's Team.

All this extracurricular activity might be received with a little better grace from us 'Boy-haters if the very proper Mr. Landry had ever raised his voice against it. Instead, when he was warned by team officials that he could lose his team to drugs, his hear-no-evil, see-no-evil approach was that his 'Boys were too close to a Super Bowl to rock the boat. The permissive tone set in the Landry era has been carried over into the Nineties. Landry may have been God's coach, and Jones, Johnson, and Switzer the Devil's own, but the value system is basically unchanged. Winning is more important than sinning.

So how sweet it was to be in the stands for Super Bowl X, rooting for the Pittsburgh Steelers as they sent the Cowboys back to Dallas on the short end, 21–17, when the balletic Lynn Swann caught a 65-yard Bradshaw pass in the closing seconds. And how we *qvelled* when Landry finally fell to 3–13 in the late Eighties and gave way to Jimmy Johnson, who went 1–15. Hey, they had fallen so low, this hating didn't come so easy anymore.

But year by year new owner Jerry Jones and new coach Jimmy Johnson brought the Cowboys back to their familiar state of domination and arrogance. The nucleus is there for yet another run at the Super Bowl. Aikman and Irvin and Smith, Neon Deion, and Ken Norton, Jr. . . . .

And we die-hard Cowboy-haters will be digging in for another season, rooting for everybody from New England to San Francisco. Go Packers! Go Patriots! Go 49ers! Go Panthers! Go Broncos!

We haven't forgotten the insensitivity of Dallas playing a football game while the country grieved for the fallen President cut down in the streets of that city, where bigotry blazoned headlines that fatal day. And we're aware of the recent NAACP attack on the Cowboys management as guilty of systematic discrimination against minorities in the front office despite a player roster that is two-thirds black.

Yes, we can even make a political case against the Cowboys. But somehow that's a little too rational for this confession of our unrelieved three decades of hatred for the Cowboys. It's bigger than politics. It's deeper than regional rivalry. And even broader than decent standards of morality.

What I'm trying to say is: If this is America's Team, I'll take Albania.

PHIL VILLAPIANO

LET ME TELL YOU something about professional football: It isn't exactly what you think it is. Nor what you see. By that I mean, when you watch the players down on the field, you are watching just one part of a two-part equation. You are watching the physical part. What you don't see is the psychological part, and that's what motivates the players. The older I get, the more I look back on the psychological part—the "rah-rah," the secret war each player has and needs—and recognize that as the most important part of the equation.

Let me try to explain. Football is the roughest, toughest, nastiest game in the world. You absolutely cannot personally like the person you're playing against and perform your job on Sunday afternoon. Doing your job properly requires you to hold them, choke them, grab them, hit them, kick them—in other words, treat them like shit. And to do so, you've got to come up with a lot of bigger-than-life reasons to do unto them before they do unto you.

There were some weeks when, on the Wednesday be-

PHIL VILLAPIANO was a linebacker for the Oakland Raiders and the Buffalo Bills from 1971 through 1983.

fore a Sunday game, I would wonder whether I was going to be mentally prepared to go out and do what I had to that weekend to win the game. It never failed. My bigger-than-life reasons would always kick in, and I would be ready. For example, I hated the 49ers because their fans called themselves the 49er "Faithful." I hated the Broncos because of the obnoxious south end zone fans, and the Colts because there were too many traffic jams getting to their stadium. I hated the Chargers because of their powder-blue sissy uniforms and because the weather was just *too* nice down there.

As you can see, I had a lot of ridiculous reasons to hate the other team. But whatever the reason, it gave me the opportunity to work myself into a lather all week over whatever team I was supposed to hate.

However, I never needed a reason to hate the Dallas Cowboys. Hating them came easily. It was a hate that went all the way back to my childhood, back to when I was in elementary school.

I was in the sixth grade the year John Kennedy ran for President. A neighbor, who was a big Kennedy supporter, even to the point of bedecking his entire house in Jack and Jackie paraphernalia, asked me to hand out buttons, bumper stickers, and anything else with the name Kennedy on it to everyone in the neighborhood. And so, every day after school, I would go door-to-door, handing out campaign material to anyone who would take it. The day Kennedy was elected, I was convinced I had single-handedly been responsible for his victory. And I wrote the new President a letter telling him of my support. Imagine my surprise when I got back a personal thank-you note, signed by him. Two and a half years later, when the tragic news came out of Dallas that Kennedy had been assassinated, I was as distraught as any eighth-grader could be. And maybe that sowed the seed for my eventual hatred of the Cowboys.

Now, jump ahead a few years. As a former player and current fan, I believe football is the only true game played, one played in any kind of weather, played anywhere, and played injured or healthy. The coaches and the referees don't matter. The only thing that matters are the teams that play. And only the best and strongest survive. Now, by the late 1960s the two best and strongest teams in pro football were the Green Bay Packers and the Dallas Cowboys—who, not incidentally, played in two of the greatest championship games in NFL history.

Just in case you don't remember the games, the first one was for the 1966 NFL championship. Dallas, down 34–20 in the fourth quarter, had come back to score and narrow Green Bay's lead to a single touchdown. And then, with less than two minutes remaining, the Cowboys had the ball and a first down on the Packers' 2-yard line. But the Pack stopped Dallas and came away with a hard-earned 34–27 victory.

The next year the two met again for the NFL championship, this time in Green Bay in what became known as "the Ice Bowl." I remember listening all week long to Don Meredith and the entire Cowboys team talking about how they were going to win this one and make up for the previous year's loss. Well, they lost this one, too, on Bart Starr's last-second quarterback sneak over Jerry Kramer's block on the goal line. Instead of Dallas taking the defeat as a tough loss, they whined and whined and whined. I hated whining then and hate it even more now that the Cowboys have perfected it to an art form.

Want another reason I hate the Cowboys? Well, in my senior year at Bowling Green I kept getting mail from Gil

Brandt of the Cowboys' front office. I would fill out those nonsensical forms time and again and return them. I remember getting real excited every time I received one. People would ask me, "Do you think you'll play in the pros?" and I would answer, "Yes, the Cowboys are writing me every day," naively believing they were sincerely interested in me. It wasn't until years later that I found out the Cowboys did the same thing to everybody, sending them all those damned forms. That really pissed me off because they had wasted my time. I don't think they ever would have drafted me. They never drafted an Italian. The closest they ever came was Tony Dorsett. At least his name *sounded* Italian.

And then there's Dallas itself. Back in the early 1970s, my Raider roomie, Bob Moore, and I had a pact, sort of a gentleman's agreement, that before every away game we would try to "culturalize" ourselves by visiting some important cultural spot in the city where we were playing—these spots could include a historical landmark, a cultural center, a restaurant, a bar, a something. After all, or so our reasoning went—he had gone to Stanford and I had gone to Bowling Green—we didn't want to waste our college education. And so it was that when the new Texas Stadium opened down there in Irving, the Raiders played the Cowboys in an exhibition game before the 1972 season. The night before the official opening of the stadium, Bob and I selected as our cultural experience Craig Morton's Bar and Restaurant. We enjoyed Craig's—and Dallas's—hospitality until the wee hours of the morning and then stumbled back to our hotel, relaxed to the max.

Well, the game wasn't just any ol' exhibition game. It was, as I said, the official opening of the new state-of-the-art Texas Stadium. The governor was there, the captains and corporals of Texas industry were there, and everybody who was anybody in the state of Texas was there. The stadium might have been pretty to look at, but I wasn't. As a matter of fact, I felt horrible and after wrestling around for a couple of plays with the interior Dallas line, I began to feel like shit. I couldn't wait for the game, which had barely begun, to end. Then, all of a sudden, I began to feel wet; a lot more than wet, soaked. I don't know how I missed it, but the stadium had no roof. And it was raining. No, not raining, pouring—almost a monsoon-like storm that had broken out on this hot, humid Texas night. On one of the first waterlogged plays after the cloudburst, a Dallas lineman came firing off the ball and hit me square in the chest, leaving me flat on my back. I remember lying there like a kid in a big mud puddle. It felt great.

I came out of the game and stood there on the sidelines, gazing up at the spectators, all sitting there nice and dry in the stands as the players went on playing. And catching pneumonia. That really pissed me off. Only in Dallas would they build a stadium with a hole in the roof. That's enough of a reason to hate Dallas.

In the mid-1970s, despite the Raiders being the most dominant team in the NFL, some know-nothings dubbed the Cowboys America's Team. And a bunch of ass-kissing writers who knew even less jumped on the bandwagon, writing crap about what a great team they were. What bullshit! We considered them a joke.

Well, it was the last game of the 1974 season, and here comes America's Team into Oakland for a *Monday Night Football* showdown. We couldn't wait to face them. Since it was tough enough playing Dallas, we didn't need the additional Monday-night garbage that usually accompanied the game. After all, we were enjoying the best record in the league, which put additional pressure on us. Before the game, coach John Madden came up with a great line, telling us: "You're never as good or as bad as the press says you are." Well, not even Howard Cosell could help America's Team that night. We beat them good, sending them and their bogus title back to Dallas, where they belonged.

I can honestly say that if the Raiders had been called America's Team, we would have turned it down. America's "Toughest Team," yes. America's "Meanest Team," probably. America's "Greatest Team," definitely. But America's Team? That crap would never have worked in Oakland.

Then there were those Dallas fans. Now, usually a player, especially a defensive player, uses crowd noise to help him know when a play is still alive or when a tackle has been made and the play's over. My job was much harder when I played in Dallas. Many's the time I'd be chasing a receiver all over the field while Roger Staubach scrambled. I wouldn't know whether to keep chasing or not because of the lack of fan reaction. I had to remember an old saying, "Don't stop until the whistle is blown." After playing there a few times, I figured Cowboy fans had no real knowledge of the game and were blinded by the bullshit of the franchise. They would rather sit around and look pretty than cheer at the right moments. I never trusted a fan with a cowboy hat, a handkerchief around his neck, and a cigar or spare rib hanging out of his mouth. They should all stay at home or go watch tennis.

Need more? By the beginning of the 1981 season, I was winding down my career with the Buffalo Bills, serving as a high-priced backup, cheerleader, and, most important of all, a control, of sorts, over Conrad Dobler. During the 1981 season we went down to play Dallas in a Monday-night game. I hadn't played in Dallas in a few years and needed to have my hatred of Dallas and Dallas fans refreshed, and to see and feel just how sickening America's Team could be at home. By halftime we were giving the Cowboys what they call down there "a good ol' ass-whuppin'." However, during the halftime break, the referees must have caught America's Team fever or something and come to the realization that the Bills should not be able to beat this mighty team. And so the third quarter featured an epidemic of yellow flags; in one stretch three were called on Conrad on three consecutive Buffalo plays, probably an all-time NFL record, for something called "leg whipping"—and then only after the Cowboys started whining. The Cowboys won, of course, courtesy of the barrage of penalty flags. And that's another reason I hate the Cowboys: Even the referees fall for that crap that America's Team can do no wrong.

In Oakland we had a saying: "Players play, coaches coach, and owners own." In short, you do the job you have, your teammates do their job, and winning will take care of itself. We had a strong coach in Oakland in John Madden, who was our leader on Sundays. We had a strong owner in Al Davis, who provided us with a first-class organization and considered us all family. In Buffalo I was fortunate enough to have another caring combination in coach Chuck Knox and owner Ralph Wilson. Both teams were a pleasure to play for.

But when I see Jerry Jones, the owner of the Cowboys, down on the field, I go ballistic. One week he's acting like a player, hugging all the Cowboys; the next week he's the coach, trying to call all the plays. I see players acting like they've never been coached and coaches doing nothing. This disorganization is bush league. And bullshit.

One last thing: I've had the privilege—no, make that the honor—of having played professional sports. And with that privilege comes something else as well: responsibility. Like it or not, when you're a professional athlete, you're a role model for millions of fans of all ages. And you have to conduct yourself in a manner that makes them look up to you and not put yourself, your team, or your league in a bad light. That's what sickens me about the Cowboys—how the NFL, the Cowboys, and the Texas authorities continue to allow members of America's Team to get away with everything and anything. In my opinion, America's Team is anything but, their off-the-field behavior and sleazy lawbreaking activities a disgrace to the sport and to everyone who follows it—including Dallas fans who don't seem to give a rap as long as they root for America's Team.

There are hundreds of NFL alumni, a lot of whom were Cowboys, who have worked hard, very hard, to make the NFL the greatest sports organization in the world. And I hate the fact that some of the current Cowboy players have betrayed the trust and responsibility they are supposed to carry and, in so doing, have undermined the work of the hundreds who went before them.

Let me end by saying that we need the Dallas Cowboys. They are an important part of football. For as in all aspects of life, we need a good guy and a bad guy. And people need to love and to hate. It makes life a more exciting journey. And the Dallas Cowboys have given us something to hate. I'm glad they're around. They've given us something to help balance our lives. They are the Team We Love to Hate, not America's Team.